Teaching Writing That Matters

Tools and Projects That Motivate Adolescent Writers

❖

Chris W. Gallagher
Amy Lee

New York • Toronto • London • Auckland • Sydney
Mexico City • New Delhi • Hong Kong • Buenos Aires

Cover design and illustration: Jorge Namerow
Interior design: LDL Designs
Acquiring editor: Gloria Pipkin
Production editor: Sarah Weaver
Copy editor: Carol Ghiglieri

ISBN-13: 978-0-545-05405-8
ISBN-10: 0-545-05405-2
Copyright © 2008 by Chris W. Gallagher and Amy Lee
All rights reserved. Published by Scholastic Inc.
Printed in the U.S.A.
1 2 3 4 5 6 7 8 9 10   23   12 11 10 09 08

Contents

Acknowledgments

We would like to thank the following people:

Our colleagues at SUNY–Albany, University of Nebraska–Lincoln, and University of Minnesota, who have contributed so much to our thinking and to this book, especially Robert Brooke, Kris Cory, Amy Goodburn, Rochelle Harris, Debbie Minter, Steve North, Joy Ritchie, and Shari Stenberg.

Our students, who continue to teach us how to teach.

Our intrepid editor, Gloria Pipkin, who helped us see that our writing mattered.

Our other editor, Lois Bridges, who makes it happen.

Our families, who supported us through this almost-decade-long project: John, Molly, Cady, and Erin. We dedicate this book to them.

Foreword

Those who can make you believe absurdities can make you commit atrocities.
—Voltaire

Education is not the filling of a pail, but the lighting of a fire.
—W. B. Yeats

There is a plague on Hogwarts School District, a darkness that has descended on the castle, not from the Death Eaters in Azkaban prison, or the devious lessons of Dark Arts teacher Severus Snape, or even the bodiless corpse of the very evil Lord Voldemort. No, this darkness came from a much more banal source: the alabaster buildings of Washington, D.C., where misguided muggle lawmakers along with a power-greedy secretive muggle administration created a law called No Child left Behind to reform the American educational system. By calling the law No Child Left Behind, the lawmakers very cleverly created a paradigm where those against the law and its impositions on creative teaching, critical thinking, and student-teacher relationships might be seen as against the progress of underprivileged children.

In reality, what the law did was give millions of dollars to testing and workbook companies, eat up hours of valuable school time with meaningless tests, and retain thousands of innocent children under the totally unfounded precept that retention will help them to learn more without all the well-documented negative-self-esteem consequences. I am not going to say how the dark lords of Washington achieved their goal, except to point out that the commonsense values of teachers and school leaders were replaced with trumped-up scientific studies funded by the same corporations that benefited from their research by selling monolithic quick-fix programs. School leaders relinquished their leadership roles and bowed to the pressure of money, politics, and the will of their superiors. There is a lack of understanding, a lack of will, a lack of hope, and a lack of courage.

Enter Harry Potter, not the brightest kid in the school, not the strongest either, and he wears spectacles to boot. But Harry has something that teachers and school leaders need more today than ever. He is creative, he is hopeful, he is kind, and he is just. But perhaps most important of all, he is *brave*.

Only a wizard like Harry Potter could have saved Hogwarts School from the darkness, and only courageous teachers with the qualities of Chris Gallagher and Amy Lee can save the American public school system from the terrible plague that NCLB has left hanging like a black shroud over our classrooms.

"This is a book of unabashed hope," says the first sentence of this incredible book. Let me repeat that so you can drink in its medicinal meaning.

"This is a book of *unabashed* hope."

Teaching Writing That Matters is a clarion call to all writing teachers everywhere to get back to real literacy instruction, back to what really will improve our schools and motivate adolescent writers. Written by two engaged, committed teachers, this important book analyzes what real writing is and shows key concepts, then demonstrates those concepts with real, practical examples of projects from middle and high school writing classrooms.

Reading this book will not only teach you how to teach meaningful writing, but also why we write and teach in the first place. Veteran and new teachers alike will be inspired by the ideas and attitude of the authors. It is a book that will be read and reworked by the teachers who use it. Like seeds, new ideas from this book will generate new writing curricula.

But though *Teaching Writing That Matters* is chock-full of practical ideas and great examples, it's not just a handbook or typical professional book. Its authors aim to inspire as much as teach. Let me repeat it one more time.

"This is a book of unabashed hope!"

Hope is that muggle ability to see past the clouds to the rainbow on the other side. Hope is the lightbulb feeling a new teacher gets at that moment when a lesson finally clicks with the students.

Hope is what turns teachers into wizards.

—*Barry Lane*

Introduction

This is a book of unabashed hope.

Not misty-eyed or head-in-the-sand hope. We're neither mystics nor prophets. We're teachers, and we come across our hope the same way most teachers do—honestly. Our teacher's hope is never unalloyed, always fragile. But without it, we would not, could not, be teachers. Our students feed on it.

For teachers today, reasons for hope sometimes seem scarce. Students often come to school alienated, disengaged, with other things on their minds (and usually with good reason, given the shape of their lives). People outside of schools, especially politicians and policymakers, exert enormous pressure on the daily life inside schools. Time, resources, and professional recognition are in short supply, even as expectations increase.

And yet here we come, peddling hope.

The source of hope we offer here goes under the unlikely name Writing Studies. Though it might sound a bit dour and academic, Writing Studies is a powerful and empowering idea. And it's an idea whose time has come.

At the college level, where we do most of our teaching, the old Freshman Comp course is being reimagined as Introduction to Writing Studies (Downs & Wardle, 2007). Instead of treating first-year writing as an all-purpose introduction to "academic discourse" or universal writing skills, college writing teachers are starting to treat it as sociologists treat Introduction to Sociology—as a course that is *about* its subject, writing. And in fact, recent collections of scholarly essays with names such as *Coming of Age* (Shamoon, Howard, Jamieson, & Schwegler, 2000), *A Field of Dreams* (O'Neill, Crow, & Burton, 2002), and *The Subject Is Writing* (Bishop & Strickland, 2006) announce that Writing Studies has arrived as a full-fledged field of study.

This development fills us, longtime writing evangelists, with hope. For many years, our work with fellow teachers has revolved around the idea that students at any level benefit from writing courses when they both study and practice writing—when it's what they *learn about* and it's what they *do*.

We first learned this lesson ourselves ten years ago, when we were teaching in a college writing program called the Writing Sequence at the State University of New York at Albany. Many teachers in the Sequence, as it was informally called, had taught traditional Freshman Comp courses with limited success. We had discovered that teaching "academic discourse"—the language and conventions of the university—was not preparing our students to write well when they left our classes because each discipline has its own language and conventions: there is no such thing as a single academic discourse. Also, as studies of intellectual "transfer" confirmed, our students were not able to transport generalized writing skills across different contexts but instead needed to build skills and familiarity within each "discourse community" they entered. It was clear to us then that the traditional Freshman Comp course, imagined as a preparatory or remedial course in generalized writing skills, was not working.

So what did we do? The almost unthinkable: we turned traditional composition inside out. Instead of treating writing as a general set of "user skills," the Sequence conceived of writing as complex intellectual work, worthy of the kind of sustained study we devote to sociology or history or engineering. Instead of treating writing as merely the "vehicle" for students' thinking about another subject, we understood it as both the means and the object of their work. In other words, students wrote in our classes, but they also *studied* writing. Instead of treating students as students who had to write, we treated them as *writers*: people who used writing for a variety of authentic purposes. Instead of pretending there are universal standards for "good writing," we taught students that "good writing" is context-specific, always a matter of negotiating the particular conventions and expectations of the writing situation. And instead of teaching Freshman Comp as remedial, an attempt to "fix" student writers, we taught it as a stimulating investigation of the work of writing and the work writing does in the world.

We knew right away that we were onto something. Students gained competence and confidence not only in our courses, but in their other courses as well. We teachers, meanwhile, were invigorated by the Writing Studies classrooms we were able to create with our students. It was scary, but also liberating, to learn new ways of interacting with students and their writing. Our weekly teaching meetings, at which we shared teaching ideas and developed the curriculum, were full of anxious excitement. We wrote and talked, talked and wrote. Often, we shared artifacts from our classrooms—assignments, responses to students, examples of student work. Sometimes we brought students into our conversations. In short, we formed a teaching and learning community that sustained our individual and collective reflection on our teaching.

Because we knew we were onto something, we began writing about the Sequence. Papers spread everywhere, we sat on the floor of Amy's apartment in Albany and began collecting our thoughts about what we and our students were experiencing. We had no idea what this project would become; we only knew we wanted to share our excitement with other teachers and their students.

Over the years, we continued to think, talk, and write about the Sequence, but a variety of other projects—many of them with our K–12 colleagues—claimed our attention as we settled into our respective homes in the Midwest.

Meanwhile, interestingly enough, the teaching of college writing was being transformed, moving toward Writing Studies.

We hope this book contributes to the development of Writing Studies. We are especially keen to share this approach with our middle school and high school teaching colleagues for two reasons. First, even if younger students are not able to conduct the kind of disciplinary inquiry that some Writing Studies proponents envision for college students,* the key tenets of Writing Studies are as appropriate for adolescents as they

---

* In fact, our own approach to teaching college writing differs in some respects from the model offered by Downs and Wardle. For instance, we do not rely as heavily as they do on empirical studies of writing, either in the reading we provide students or the research we ask them to conduct. Though we do introduce students to research on writing and ask them to study writing, what is most important to us is that they come to see themselves as *writers* participating in a variety of personally meaningful "discourse communities," rather than *scholars* confined to the discourse community of Writing Studies itself.

are for young adults. It is never too early for students to think of themselves, or for us to think of them, as writers. Nor is it ever too early to investigate with students how writing works and the work it does in the world.

Second, on a more personal note, we spend a great deal of time working with and learning from our colleagues in middle and secondary schools, and so it is important to us to invite them into the Writing Studies conversation. For us, Writing Studies is an invigorating, hopeful, even joyful idea about teaching and learning writing. Whether you teach middle school, high school, or college, we invite you to explore it with us.

> **It is never too early for students to think of themselves, or for us to think of them, as writers.**

To that end, we have designed this book to be interactive. In addition to providing lots of tools and projects for Writing Studies classrooms, we offer you the opportunity to do the kind of thinking and writing that you ask of your students. We encourage you to write alongside your students because, as the old National Writing Project adage has it, "The best teachers of writing are writers themselves." The activities in this book could be completed in collaboration with colleagues as part of a professional learning community, inquiry group, workshop, or class. Alternatively, you could keep a personal notebook for your writing or simply reflect on the activities. We believe these activities are rich enough to get (and keep) you thinking in productive ways even if you simply devote a few moments' thought to them as you read.

Chapter 1 sets the stage for the rest of the book. It explores the state of teaching and writing in schools today and makes the case for careful reflection on the joys and torments of these important activities, which have so much in common. Chapter 2 extends this discussion by exploring what we call "testing despair," an affliction that must be acknowledged and treated in today's educational reality. But despair need not be a permanent condition.

Taking a close look at the most problematic forms of testing writing allows us to develop a fresh view of what we and our students need in order to become engaged and effective teachers and writers: *reflective practice, rhetorical awareness,* and a *sense of community*. Chapters 3–5, which form Part II, are organized around these three key Writing Studies concepts. Each of these chapters includes activities for teachers and for students, as well as discussion of why these concepts are the building blocks of teaching and writing that matter. These chapters are predicated on concepts that are receiving a great deal of attention in the emerging Writing Studies literature, but we distill the ideas and make them accessible and usable for any teacher who wishes to motivate her students to write with confidence, competence, and above all, consequence.

> Taking a close look at the most problematic forms of testing writing allows us to develop a fresh view of what we and our students need in order to become engaged and effective teachers and writers: *reflective practice, rhetorical awareness*, and a *sense of community*.

Part III presents three project toolboxes full of classroom-tested project ideas and supplemental tools for writers, one writer's process toolbox with general tools that you will find useful for guiding your students through any type of project, and one teacher's toolbox with tools designed to help you develop as a reflective writing teacher. The project toolboxes are organized around the kinds of intellectual work that writers do: writing *with* experience, writing *with* texts, and writing *with* research. These categories parallel common "modes" of writing in schools (expository/narrative, analysis, and research, respectively), but our emphasis is less on helping students generate a "kind" of writing than on helping them develop into reflective, rhetorically aware, community-minded writers who write for real, meaningful purposes and audiences both inside and outside the classroom.

Though Parts II and III are chock-full of activities and tools we and our colleagues have used to build our own classrooms, and we hope many of them will be useful as you build yours, there is no One Right Way to write or to teach. Notwithstanding the hundreds of "best practices" books thrown at teachers each year, all the tools in the world will not be much help to a builder who doesn't know what she is building—or who doesn't want to build anything. Our fondest hope for this book, then, is not that it will build a classroom for you, but rather that it will help you build your own classrooms in which you teach and your students write with confidence, competence, and consequence.

PART I

Toward Writing Studies Classrooms

Chapter 1

The Joys (and Torments) of Teaching and Writing

Learning to write is hard, and it takes a long time.
—Steve North

In *The Writing Life*, Annie Dillard (1989) complains that too many writers fail to cover their tracks—fail, as she puts it, to "tie off the umbilical cord." She asks, "Is it pertinent, is it courteous, for us to learn what it cost the writer personally?" (p. 7).

Maybe not. And yet, as writers, and even more so as writing teachers, we know what a powerful and instructive gift it is to be invited into another's creative process, to understand—as Dillard herself helps us to understand in her book—how writing comes to be.

And so we begin—perhaps impertinently, discourteously—by *un*covering our tracks, refusing to tie off the umbilical cord. We begin by telling you this: learning to write this book was hard, and it took a long time.

Of course, we should have known this; learning to write *anything* has always been hard work for us, and we regularly counsel our students to develop the patience and discipline this fickle art of writing requires. And yet, when it comes to writing, we are like the baby who is surprised *every time* that loved one reappears from behind her own hands.

Who knew that we would have to learn to write this book by . . . writing this book?

Among all the insights we share with our students about writing, this one seems particularly crucial: writing teaches writers how to write—and how not to write.

We think of ourselves as proficient writers. Certainly we have had lots of experience—and some success: each of us has published books and articles. And yet, with this project, we made nearly endless mistakes and false starts. We also had what seemed like more than our share of tough days, when the writing just wouldn't come or when it felt like we were writing in circles.

> **Writing teaches writers how to write—and how not to write.**

In this way, writing is a lot like teaching. We've had plenty of tough teaching days, too. Some days seem like torture. We slog through our lessons, sure that nothing is sticking, certain that we're not the teachers we could be—or half the teacher that hotshot next door is on a bad day.

Just as our young writers need to learn patience with themselves, so too do we need to be patient with our teaching selves. And just as writers learn to write only by writing and reflecting on that writing, teachers learn to teach only by teaching and reflecting on that teaching. In both cases, there are no secret formulas or foolproof plans that will help us "arrive"; we are always *becoming* writers and teachers.

On bad days, this all seems awfully dispiriting; who would knowingly subject themselves to this kind of pain? But we get through the tough days because we know that if we keep working, keep thinking, the good days will come. We know that bad teaching and bad writing—when well reflected on—can lead to good teaching and good writing. And when those good days do come, they can be pure exhilaration. The victories might be small and infrequent, but they are joyful.

Joy is not a word we hear often these days to describe either writing or teaching. No one doubts the importance of these activities; we hear all the time that "highly qualified teachers" are the most important factor in helping children learn and that writing is a "gateway for success in academia, the new workplace, and the global economy, as well as for our collective success as a participatory democracy" (Nagin, 2003, p. 1; see also Graham & Perin's Carnegie report *Writing Next* [2006] and the National Commission on Writing, 2003, 2004, 2005, 2006). But despite widespread agreement that we must get better at writing and teaching writing, we don't hear much about the exquisite joys and torments they hold. In fact, few people talk about *what it's like* to write and teach—how we experience these activities, how they feel.

This, we will argue, is a huge problem. Perhaps because ours is a get-it-done-yesterday culture, we seem to have lost touch with *writing* and *teaching* as verbs; instead, we focus all our energy on their noun forms. As a result, too few young people feel empowered to claim writing as an important part of their lives, particularly in school, and too few teachers feel empowered to claim teaching as their professional prerogative. There seems to be no room, and no time, to write and teach in ways that really *matter*.

There are reasons for this sad state of affairs, and we believe most of them have little to do with choices teachers and students make, despite the familiar rhetoric of "low expectations" in schools. We believe it is important to confront these reasons, and that is one of the aims of this book. But our ultimate aim—the one that kept us going through our toughest writing days—is to help you teach, and help your students write, in ways that matter.

Having Something to Say

What do we mean when we talk about teaching or writing that *matters*? More than a hundred years ago, John Dewey penned a line that we believe should be taped above every writer's—and every teacher's—desk: "There is all the difference in the world between having something to say and having to say something" (1956/1900, p. 67). *Mattering* in teaching and writing is all about having something to say—even if we do *have* to say something.

This was the all-important lesson that we had to relearn with this very project. There was a moment, on the long and winding road to this book, when we almost lost our way. We were initially working with a different editor and publisher

> "There is all the difference in the world between having something to say and having to say something."
> — John Dewey

who were, understandably, extremely concerned about the "marketability" of the book. We felt pressure to "dumb down" the book, given the publisher's disappointing assumptions about and estimation of teachers (our target audience) and what "they" want. We had been granted a contract based on our proposal for a book that tried new things—a more personal writing voice, an innovative structure, edgy writing assignments. So we were confused later when this seemed to be the opposite of what our editor wanted: a more conventional, more "mainstream" book.

As we fumbled our way toward a new version of the project—that is, as the project drifted further from our own vision of it—we noticed something at once interesting and terrifying: our writing became worse and worse. Those writing days truly were torture. We generated garbled sentences and grotesque paragraphs. Our arguments became tangled, our logic warped. Sometimes, our writing didn't make sense even to us.

We liken this experience to situations we've faced as teachers when our expertise and commitment were neither valued nor welcome—situations, for example, where "outcomes" were handed to us without our input. When we do not have a stake in our own teaching, when our hard-won professional judgment is not honored, our teaching suffers. We lack confidence, we go through the motions, we become defensive, and in general, we behave in ways that violate our sense of our own professionalism. (Studies of teaching under high-stakes standardized testing bear this out; see, for example, McNeil, 2000).

Fortunately, our story has a happy ending. Though it took us longer than it should have, we finally realized that we could not write well if we did not believe in our project and if we did not believe that someone on the other side of the page actually wanted to hear what we had to say. We could not write well when we *had* to say something because we were under contract and not because we had something to say. Eventually, we found a new editor and a new publisher who shared our vision for the book. When this happened, we were able to recapture our initial excitement for this project. In turn, our writing improved—became more purposeful, meaningful, forceful, and clear.

Our experience bears out writing teacher Linda Brodkey's reminders that "writing is not a spectator sport" and that "learning *how to write* follows from *wanting to write*"

(1996, p. 51, emphasis hers). And we would say the same about teaching. Effective teachers want to be in the classroom and believe they and their students have important things to say to one another and to others.

Having to Say Something

Unfortunately, in schools, teachers and students often feel stifled, as if they do not have a voice. Teachers are handed instructional scripts to read and told to "cover" curriculum at a predetermined pace. Students are told to produce writing on demand for the purpose of evaluation; they write, sure, but only as students, never as writers.

It's true, of course, that we must grade and otherwise evaluate student writing. But the problem occurs when we place so much emphasis on this extrinsic reward (or punishment) and lose sight of the fact that we humans do our most creative and effective work when we are driven by an intrinsic motivation: a human need to investigate, to wonder, to imagine, to share, to teach, to persuade, to learn.

And it's a serious problem, too, because as our own story of writing this book shows, extrinsic motivations often get in the way of intrinsic ones. In our case, an editor with an agenda and a looming contract deadline interfered with our ability to sustain our commitment to a project to which we had already given years of thought and care. It's not hard to see, then, how our students might find it difficult to sustain interest in and commitment to their school work in the face of teachers' and others' agendas and grading systems.

The trick, it seems to us, is to create environments in which we nurture intrinsic motivation, even if all we have direct access to are extrinsic ones (we can't

> We do our most creative and effective work when we are driven by an intrinsic motivation: a human need to investigate, to wonder, to imagine, to share, to teach, to persuade, to learn.

make people care, the sad old adage goes). That's what our new editor did for us as writers: she helped us recapture our latent excitement for and commitment to our own work. She did this primarily by taking us seriously, by offering us supportive and sometimes challenging responses to our ideas, and above all by showing us that our writing *mattered*. (It should not surprise you to learn that she was previously a longtime middle school teacher.) Like a good teacher, our editor kept us focused on *having something to say*, even if, under our new contract, we *had to say something*.

This, we suggest, is the toughest challenge of teaching in schools today. While almost all of us do want to hear what students have to say, and chose the profession in large part for that very reason, our culture and our educational systems are sadly not very good at listening—to students or to teachers. All too often, important decisions about teaching and learning don't take place in classrooms, or even in schools, but in conference rooms downtown and boardrooms who knows where. Interactions between teachers and students are governed by checklists, guidelines, rubrics, lists of outcomes and objectives and competencies and standards, prepackaged curricula, scripts, and of course standardized tests. In many schools today, what teachers and students have to say seems irrelevant. Everyone's too busy covering the curriculum in time for the next round of tests anyway. Who has time even to figure out what we have to say?

But here's the thing: the potential cost of *not* reflecting, of not figuring out what we and our students have to say and then saying it, is astronomical. We risk losing what is most important in teaching and learning: the kinds of relationships we form with young people. Top-down policies, prepackaged curriculum, scripted instruction, all-important (and all-imported) standardized tests—these send the message that teachers are mere "delivery systems" and students are merely "consumers" of other people's knowledge and skills, or worse: they are "products" to which we "add value" in preparation for the marketplace (see Meier, 2002; Gallagher, 2007).

What does all this mean for writing?

Let us introduce you to Michelle. Michelle is a first-year college student. On the basis of her high school grades and especially her very high test scores, she has been admitted to the Honors Program at her state university. Her academic scholarships pay most of her way, but she needs some spending money. So she peruses the university's online employment page and notices a student worker job in the Writing Center. It sounds like an interesting opportunity, so she decides to apply. She copies the e-mail address of the contact name on the ad—which happens to be Chris Gallagher, Coordinator of Composition—and pastes it into her e-mail program. She composes and sends the following e-mail:

> hey chris
> i saw the job you posted for english and it sounds like fun!! how do i apply for it? i think i'd be really good at it! *?*
> michelle

Now Michelle may be very bright, and a good test taker to boot. Our guess is that like most of her peers, Michelle is probably adept at instant messaging, texting, blogging, and all manner of instant (or nearly instant) communication. She probably knows all the lingo: *bff* for "best friends forever," *g2g* for "got to go," *lol* for "laugh out loud," and so on. In fact, she's probably writing all day long.

But clearly, Michelle lacks "rhetorical awareness"—a concept we'll have a lot to say about in this book, but which essentially means an understanding of how to write in *this* situation, for *this* audience, for *this* purpose. She is writing in precisely the way she probably writes all the time, seemingly unaware that she needs to adjust her writing for different contexts.

It's easy to wish Michelle just knew better—that she saw her extremely informal approach as an obvious *faux pas*. But Michelle likely has had few opportunities to write in meaningful, reflective ways and to develop into an agile writer. Probably she has had few opportunities to participate in forums in which people grow their ideas together through careful, thoughtful reflection and conversation.

In fact, despite the proliferation of online communication spaces, the print and physical spaces in which young people might write in ways that matter—ways that make a difference in their lives and communities—are shrinking. Spaces that were at one time public are rapidly being privatized, and media outlets are consolidating left and right. Citizens, and especially young people, have fewer and fewer avenues in which to have a voice in public deliberations. As writing teacher Nancy Welch (2005) suggests, in our age, searching, democratic public debate has largely given way to closed-door decision making by a small group of elites who control the bulk of our economic and cultural resources.

Is it really surprising, then, that so many of our young college students are like Michelle: smart, passionate, engaging . . . and virtually clueless about how to write outside of highly constrained, prescriptive classroom and testing situations? Surely, if you put a test prompt in front of Michelle and set the timer, she would perform—she knows how to produce fast writing. But at what cost has she been trained to do this, and this alone?

The Hope of *Teaching Writing That Matters*

Despite this dire state of affairs, this book emerges from a stubborn faith in teachers, in students, and in the power of Writing Studies classrooms. We've written the book because we believe that students can write and teachers can teach in ways that matter—ways that make a difference in their own and others' lives. We believe students and teachers can have something to say even if they have to say something. We believe they can be responsive to the varied writing and teaching opportunities that present themselves. And we believe that writing classrooms can be exciting places where teachers and students *want* to be and where, as a result, they do their best work.

For that to happen, we teachers need to engage in serious, deliberative, and collective reflection about what drives our teaching. We need to refuse the idea that reflection is a luxury and claim it not only as our professional prerogative, but as our birthright as human beings. We need to figure out what we have to say, and then we have to say it. We need to ground ourselves in

> We believe that students can write and teachers can teach in ways that matter— ways that make a difference in their own and others' lives.

our own beliefs about writing and teaching writing. We need to capture, or recapture, some simple truths about writing and teaching—why we do these things, what we believe about them, what it feels like to do them, their torments and their joys.

> We need to refuse the idea that reflection is a luxury.

If we manage to do these things, we just might find ourselves teaching, and our students writing, with confidence, competence, and consequence. That is the promise of Writing Studies; that is the hope of *Teaching Writing That Matters.*

Chapter 2

Testing Despair and Teaching Hope

Meet Lisa, Chris's friend and neighbor:

"I just can't stand what I'm made to do to kids every day," she says. "I know it's not right. It's all testing, testing, testing. Where's the learning? Where's the excitement? Where's the joy? It's not right, what we do to these kids."

After fifteen years teaching at a diverse, high-poverty middle school, Lisa is "worn down." She still loves the job, loves the students, but it is hard, she says, "to do well all the things teachers need to do." This includes the escalating and now nearly continuous administration of tests, which has crowded out the hands-on, inquiry-based learning she and her students loved. When she's not administering tests, she is rushing to "cover" the tested material, often through seat work instead of the more time-consuming but engaging projects and experiments she and her students once did all the time.

Drained by the demands of the classroom but as committed as ever to helping students learn, Lisa has taken the necessary coursework to become a media specialist. Fortunately for her, that position opened up at her school, so she is staying on. Lisa is hopeful that being released from the strictures of a lockstep curriculum and pencil-and-paper tests will allow her to interact with students in ways she believes adults should interact with young people in schools: authentically and with full attention. As she moves into the media center, she thinks of herself as entering a larger classroom—one in which she looks forward to helping young people grow and to growing professionally herself.

We applaud Lisa's commitment to students and her stand against what she considers professional malpractice. We're glad she's not following the lead of many of her colleagues and leaving the profession altogether—even though we understand why smart, committed people often find teaching stifling in this age of testing.

Chris has written elsewhere about the "testing despair" epidemic afflicting the teaching profession (Gallagher, 2007). We suspect you understand what we're talking about: that hot-fist feeling you get in your chest when, in the name of high test scores, you are made to do something to your students that you *know* is not good for them; when you are routinely made to violate your teacherly instincts and what you believe about teaching and learning in order to satisfy an anonymous, remote bureaucracy; when you realize that the tail (testing) is wagging the dog (teaching), and you are part of a system that either doesn't recognize that fact or doesn't care.

In this chapter, we explain how the kind of on-demand, standardized writing tests common in most states and districts across the country deny students and teachers what they most need in order to write and teach writing in ways that matter: *reflection*, *rhetorical awareness*, and a *sense of community*.* These are the three key concepts we will explore in Part II.

How Testing Thwarts Reflection

In his informative but depressing book *The Testing Trap*, George Hillocks (2002) studies five state writing assessments from different parts of the U.S. and concludes that, for the most part, they encourage formulaic writing, impoverished writing pro-

---

* We are *not* arguing against all assessment, or even testing. Assessment is simply the process of gathering information about what students know and can do—something teachers do every day. It need not take the form of a test. Testing, meanwhile, comes in many forms and has its place in a comprehensive approach to assessment. What we're concerned with in this chapter are standardized, timed, impromptu writing tests.

grams, and rote, unimaginative teaching. What we find most valuable about Hillocks's work is his attention to the often implicit "theory of writing" that informs these tests, and how that theory, when put into practice through a test, shapes how teachers "think about the nature of writing and learning and the kind of learning environment they create" (p. 21).

Here's an example. Many state policymakers have decided to test three "domains" or "modes" of writing: expository, narrative, and persuasive. As Hillocks notes, the rationale here is that together these three "domains" offer a comprehensive view of writing (p. 40). Presumably, we are dealing with *purposes* for writing: it provides information, tells a story, or makes an argument.

But we know that most good writing does more than one of these things at a time. An effective television commercial may be said to be primarily persuasive, but even a 30-second ad tells a story and provides information about its product. A compelling novel may be said to be narrative, but it must convince us to "believe" in the world it creates, and it would be impossible to do this without providing information. Even a straightforward set of instructions—seemingly strictly informational—tells a story of how to assemble a product and tries to convince us (often unsuccessfully, in our experience) that *this* is the best way to do it.

But the theory of writing underpinning these state writing tests insists that these categories are real and distinct, and that if we have students write in each of the three—say, narrative in fourth grade, expository in eighth, and persuasive in twelfth—then we've "covered" the universe of discourse. Never mind the flawed theory of development here—the idea that telling stories is more elemental than giving information, which is simpler than making arguments. Focus instead on how we end up presenting writing to students. In eighth grade, for instance, we might tell them to write "a description." But do writers ever sit down with the sole intention of writing a description? Sure, writers describe things all the time—just as they tell stories and provide information. But these are things writers do as means to their chosen ends, not ends in themselves. A fiction writer describes a graveyard so as to foreshadow the protagonist's impending death. But she does not decide one day out of the blue to sit down and describe a graveyard. And she certainly doesn't accomplish that description by doing an exercise to determine what a graveyard would taste, smell, look, feel, and sound like. But that's the kind of thing teachers in eighth-grade classrooms across the country have their students do all the time: "Here is an object. Now list ten describing words for each of the five senses." If a student has the temerity to ask why they are doing this, the teacher might give a generic answer about the importance of concrete detail, but the *real* answer has everything to do with the test: the students will need to write "a description." When put together with the narrative they wrote back in fourth grade and the persuasion they will write in a few years, they will have a complete writing education.

So, because the theory of writing held by people in a state office building holds that writing has separate but complementary "domains," teachers in eighth-grade classrooms end up running their students through endless exercises in generating sensory details about random objects. Whether or not it is explicit—most often it is not—there is a theory of writing here. There is also a theory of learning that says that breaking writing down into constituent parts is the best way to learn how to do it. And there's a theory of teaching here, too, which holds that skill-based exercises are the best way to teach students to write.

We could go on and on about the assumptions and values implicit in all this. But our point, following Hillocks, is that the tests *do* rest on theories of writing, teaching, and learning, and that these theories shape what happens in writing classrooms.

Let's take this one step further. Hillocks notes that while many teachers he interviewed didn't like certain aspects of the state tests, they were ill-equipped to offer detailed critiques because they lacked training in the academic field of composition and rhetoric, and as a result, the tests *became* the theory of writing informing their teaching (p. 198). We agree with Hillocks—to a point. Chris's research on a state writing assessment found something similar: teachers often lack a language to describe their discomfort with and objections to the test. He also found that what gets tested—in this case the familiar "six traits of writing"—sometimes becomes the curriculum. For example, teachers spend two weeks on voice, another two on organization, another two on sentence fluency, and so on. But he also found that most teachers, even those who did not know how to articulate their ideas about the test, understood and resented the limitations of the test. The theory underlying the test might have become the theory driving their classroom practice, even though many teachers did not agree with the theory. Instead, they were far more likely to acquiesce to it because they did not see other options if they wanted their students to succeed.

Our difference with Hillocks here might seem slight, but we believe it is important. If we frame the problem as a lack of training in composition and rhetoric—or Writing Studies, as we prefer to call our field—then the solution, clearly, is to provide more teachers with that training. We believe that would be a valuable endeavor; in fact, we see this book as one attempt to introduce our readers to the idea of Writing Studies. But we don't think it's enough. Surely it would be to teachers' advantage to be equipped with the theory that helps explain the shortcomings of standardized writing tests. But as important as it is to understand how the tests violate what writing research and theory tell us about teaching and learning writing, it is at least as important to reflect on how they violate our own considered experiences and beliefs as writers and teachers of writing. What we really need are *reflective practitioners*: thoughtful teachers who make it a habit to inquire into their own experiences and beliefs and who ground their practice in that ongoing inquiry. (Interestingly, this is a key tenet in the field of Writing Studies; see also Schön, 1987.) A well-trained teacher, armed with the most cutting-edge theory and research, will not be able to withstand the erosive (often corrosive) power of top-down school cultures and the political pressures that support these tests unless she is working from a sound foundation of strongly held and well-considered beliefs (Wilson, 1994).

The weight of history and tradition—"the way we do things around here"—helps explain why despite three decades of research supporting process-based instruction, the primary instructional

> What we really need are *reflective practitioners*: thoughtful teachers who make it a habit to inquire into their own experiences and beliefs and who ground their practice in that ongoing inquiry.

mode in most secondary English classrooms remains what John Goodlad (1984) famously called "frontal," or what Hillocks (2002) calls "presentational." That is, the predominant classroom activities have remained constant over time: lecture, recitation (rote questioning and answering), and skills-building exercises (see also Nystrand, 1997). "Teach Process, Not Product" has been the rallying cry of composition and rhetoric at least since 1972, when Donald Murray published an article with that title. But despite the near-unanimity this idea has enjoyed among those who study and teach writing, it is often not put into practice in writing classrooms. Indeed, given the ubiquity and authority of writing tests that privilege writing products—writing that matches the "product descriptors" on rubrics—there is perhaps less attention to writing process in U.S. classrooms today than ever before. And it's not because teachers have turned their backs on the process movement; most of us believe in the importance of process. Rather, it's because the tests have rendered our beliefs about writing and teaching irrelevant.

These tests, then, cut teachers off from the kind of reflection that is the hallmark of our professionalism. But it's not just that the theory of the tests replaces teachers' knowledge and beliefs. In many cases, it runs counter to them, leaving teachers in a constant state of conflict. And the more thoughtful the teacher, the more painful this disconnect between what she wants for her students and what she's made to do to her students. Call it Lisa's Dilemma.

Meanwhile, as Lisa recognizes, these tests limit and circumscribe students' reflective thinking as well. Students are made to write on demand for a specified (and typically short) period of time on a topic they have been handed, without the opportunity to conduct inquiry or even the time needed to deliberate carefully. The testing conditions create what Hillocks aptly calls "truncated thinking." And because classroom practices so often approximate testing conditions—we understandably want our students to pass the tests—teachers wind up teaching truncated thinking. Teachers and students alike, then, are cut off from the kind of reflective thinking that most teachers entered the profession to share with young people.

How Testing Thwarts Rhetorical Awareness

The writing that students produce under the conditions just described, even at the highest score points on rubrics, is typically what our college students impolitely but accurately call "bullshit." The writing may be clear, concise, and well organized, but it often doesn't say anything.

Let's examine an actual example. The following is a sample student-generated essay used by the Nebraska Department of Education. It was used to train scorers of an eleventh-grade statewide assessment, to show them what a "4"—the highest score point—looks like. The prompt for the essay was this: "Assume that the Nebraska legislature is considering a bill that would prohibit high school students from working at after-school jobs during the school year. 1—Determine your position on this proposal. 2—In a persuasive essay, present your opinions and provide specific examples to support it."

> The Nebraska Legislature is considering a bill that would prohibit high school students from working at after-school jobs during the school year. I am against this proposal because after-school jobs provide work experience for future jobs, teach students to manage time, and give students the opportunity to use money wisely.
>
> First, I am against this proposal because it takes away from work experience for future jobs. Many of the basic job skills come from part-time jobs that took place while that person was in high school. If this bill was passed, students would not receive the hands-on experience required in professional or non-professional job areas.
>
> Secondly, I am against this proposal because part-time jobs teach students to manage their time wisely. Many students hold after-school jobs and receive very good grades in school. I put in about 20 hours a week after school at my job, and I still manage to be top ranked in my class. After-school jobs tell students to work harder at homework while in school, because their out-of-school time will be spent at work.

Finally, I am against this proposal because after-school jobs give students the opportunity to use money wisely. Some students get jobs because they want to save money for college. Other students want to buy a new vehicle and need a source of income. By setting financial goals, an after school job can help accomplish these goals if the students decides to spend and save their money wisely.

All in all, I am against this proposal because it takes away experience from students in high school who are looking forward to a college education or have set financial goals for themselves. An after-school job teaches students skills that are necessary in the work force.

(Nebraska Department of Education, 2001)

This piece of writing has a lot going for it. It is clear, focused, and carefully organized. It is an almost perfect example of the classic five-paragraph theme. But while the writer shows a certain facility with language, the writing is, well, facile. Generalities build upon each other: "Many of the basic job skills come from part-time jobs that took place while that person was in high school. If this bill was passed, students would not receive the hands-on experience required in professional or non-professional job areas." Which skills? How do they "come from" these jobs? What experience? Are skills and experience the same thing? Are the skills mentioned here different from or inclusive of the ones discussed in the ensuing paragraphs? Why would passage of the bill—which would prohibit working after-school jobs only during the school year—mean students would not get work experience? Where is the evidence to support these claims?

Even a gentle poke at the logic of the argument reveals problems. The final sentence of the third paragraph, for instance, seems to unravel the argument presented in that paragraph: "After-school jobs tell students to work harder at homework while in school, because their out-of-school time will be spent at work." This sentence bluntly states that students with after-school jobs will not do homework at home—an argument not likely to win over many readers. But it also makes a questionable logical leap: if students cannot do homework at home, then they will work harder to get it done in school. Similarly, the next paragraph claims that "after-school jobs give students the opportunity to use money wisely." Fair enough. But don't they also give students the opportunity to use money *un*wisely? Perhaps recognizing this potential problem, the writer ends the paragraph with a convoluted rewriting of the first sentence: "By setting financial goals, an after-school job can help accomplish these goals if the students decides [sic] to spend and save their time wisely." The grammar of the sentence is telling: The writer seems to recognize mid-sentence that it is not the job that accomplishes the goals, but rather the students, who may or may not spend their money wisely.

We don't mean to pick on this student writer (or, by the way, on Nebraska, which is a national leader in assessment, as Chris has written about extensively). In fact, we applaud her. She seems to know just the kind of writing the test invites, and she delivers. In fact, it may be said that this piece succeeds precisely because it is fast writing for fast-reading scorers; this student is writing to be evaluated, not read. After all, this student is (strangely enough) writing a "persuasive essay" about a policy being considered by her state legislature. That she isn't being asked to write, say, an article or an editorial for a student newspaper or a letter to a legislator seems almost perverse. The writers of this prompt had to work pretty hard to make sure the students didn't write anything that anyone might actually write in the real world.

Speaking of the real world, consider how realistic this prompt seemed to the students on a particular Native American reservation that Chris visited. This community struggled with dire poverty; its unemployment rate hovered around 75 percent, and 99 percent of its students had free or reduced lunch. In a community in which the vast majority of adults have no jobs at all, it is not hard to see why so many high school students did not even understand the prompt. Several students wrote something along the lines of "There are no jobs here, period" and left it at that.

Our point is that meaningful writing is *always* contextual; it takes place in a specific place for a specific purpose for a specified audience. Effective writers write with their purpose, audience, and context in mind; they are, in the parlance of Writing Studies, "rhetorically aware." These tests, on the other hand, either try to "neutralize" context, as the above prompt does, or they ignore it altogether: "Describe your favorite object." "Tell about a time things didn't work out like you thought they would."

"Explain the three most important qualities of a great leader." If one were to ask *why* and *for whom* students write, the only honest answer is, "to be evaluated by scorers." And yet, without a sense of why and for whom one is writing, it is difficult for any writer to produce work that isn't trite and meaningless—to produce writing that matters.

This is perhaps the worst message we can send students about writing. It tells them, in effect, that their ideas are unimportant and that the person on the other side of the page does not care about what they have to say, beyond assigning a number.

Teachers, meanwhile, must teach students to write in ways that bear no resemblance to the behavior of people who actually write. Teaching itself becomes standardized. Teachers are routinely handed rubrics that tell them, before their students ever set foot in their classrooms, what "good writing" looks like. And they are made to run endless "practice tests," handing students prompts, timing them, and then scoring their "answers." Recently, some publishers—presumably in an effort to ease overworked teachers' heavy workloads, and under the predictable guise of "best practices"—have gotten into the game by producing handy comment charts that teachers can give to their students or post in their classrooms. A student struggling to develop ideas, for instance, might have "D6" written on his in-class draft. Using his chart, he will see that "D6" means "Use at least one concrete Detail in each paragraph." That this tool saves time seems indisputable; that it impoverishes the dialogue between student and teacher—perhaps our most important classroom resource—seems equally undeniable.

The truth is, both writing and teaching are rhetorical acts; that is, both are shaped by our purposes, audiences, and contexts. That's because they are relational arts—ways in which we connect with other people. But in the name of efficiency—controlled conditions, quick reads, simple scores—standardized impromptu writing exams ignore all this, actively suppressing rhetorical awareness.

> **Effective writers write with their purpose, audience, and context in mind; they are, in the parlance of Writing Studies, "rhetorically aware."**

How Testing Thwarts a Sense of Community

Relational acts—acts of human engagement—take on meaning, significance, and consequence only in the contexts in which people care about and are responsive to each other's efforts. They are accomplished primarily and most effectively through conversation, through the exchange of information, ideas, and values—in short, in community.

In her book *In Schools We Trust*, Deborah Meier (2002) argues convincingly that our first responsibility as teachers is to help students learn "the art of democratic conversation" (p. 4). Schools are, or should be, places where students learn how to talk and how to listen, how to reason, how to deliberate, how to persuade, and how to be persuaded. This is the essence of learning. And it's the essence of teaching, too: "One teaches best by listening," Meier writes (p. 23). For Meier, and for us, teaching and learning in a diverse democracy are all about learning to live well together. And we can only do this if we are fully present for our students and they are fully present for each other.

Likewise, writers need readers—and other writers—who are fully present for them. Although some of our cultural myths perpetuate the idea that reading and writing are purely individual acts—think of the white-haired writer pounding away on a typewriter in his lonely attic or the solitary figure sitting under a tree with her book—they are, as Deborah Brandt (1990) points out, "pure acts of human involvement" (p. 6). And so, Brandt suggests, "learning to read is learning that you are being written to, and learning to write is learning that your words are being read" (p. 5).

> Schools are, or should be, places where students learn how to talk and how to listen, how to reason, how to deliberate, how to persuade, and how to be persuaded.

Learners, writers, and teachers all need a sense of community, connection with other human beings based on a shared interest or endeavor, in order to grow. They need to know that they have something to say—and that others are listening. But standardized, on-demand writing tests offer us just the opposite. Students are not writing to be read; they are writing to be evaluated. And teachers are not reading; they are scoring. Writing is not conversation; it is performance.

Indeed, most testing protocols call conversation among writers "cheating." Teachers cannot talk to their students and students cannot talk to each other about the writing they are doing. Again, in addition to being inauthentic—writers talk with other writers and readers all the time—this prohibition sacrifices a crucial component of learning in the name of a faulty conception of "ability." The idea here is that we want a "true measure" of each individual's "competence." And so we attempt to strip away all outside factors. But even if it were possible to discount contextual factors—and we doubt that it is—what we're left with doesn't tell us anything meaningful about student writing because writing is always a contextual act. So not only have we not measured what we wanted to measure, but we've robbed students—and teachers—of the opportunity to become members of supportive communities.

Conclusion

In order to grow, teachers and writers need to become reflective practitioners of their art, to be rhetorically aware, and to have the support of a community. But the way we test writing in schools does not encourage—and in many ways actively discourages—these developments. No wonder we see such rampant testing despair; as Lisa understands, teachers and students alike are systematically disconnected from that which would nourish their work.

And yet, we remain hopeful. On the political level, we see teachers and students (and often their parents) working together to resist high-stakes standardized testing and to reclaim their schools and classrooms (Gallagher, 2007). Just as importantly, we find hope in the emerging model of Writing Studies and in the exciting classrooms of our secondary and postsecondary colleagues, many of whom have helped us craft the projects and tools in Parts II and III of this book. In particular, we are buoyed by what we see as the re-emergence of reflection, rhetorical awareness, and community in writing instruction today. The next three chapters take up these key concepts in turn.

PART II

❖

Key Concepts for Teaching and Writing

Chapter 3

Reflection in Teaching and Writing

Meet Kendra:

Sitting silently at her desk, she stares at the blank page in front of her. The class is now three minutes into its five-minute freewriting activity in which students are supposed to describe, as quickly and in as much detail as they can, a "scene of writing": a visual image they have of a writer writing. The idea is to unearth the internalized images and ideas about writing and writers that students bring with them to college. But Kendra and her pencil sit quiet, motionless.

Amy shuffles over to Kendra. Before she can ask if everything is okay, Kendra whispers quietly but firmly: "I can't do it."

"Write," Amy whispers back, "Just write anything that comes to mind."
A moment passes. Kendra frowns.

Finally, she says: "But I don't have *any scenes of writing in my mind. I never picture anyone writing. I don't know anyone who writes if they don't have to. I mean, why would they?"*

Kendra was a 17-year-old African American first-generation college student. She graduated from an urban high school with a graduation rate of only 53 percent. Eighty percent of the students in the high school were students of color, but in the university, she found herself in a small minority. In her high school, Kendra was a solid, even exceptional student; in fact, she was among the 10 percent who would go on to higher education. But as a college student, she was identified as "remedial" on the basis of admissions criteria and placement tests.

As a result of these shifts, Kendra struggled mightily during her first semester of college. In Amy's basic writing course, she was befuddled by texts that challenged traditional conceptions of schooling—Theodore Sizer's analogy between high schools and supermarkets in "What High School Is" (1984), for example, and Paulo Freire's notion of "banking" education in *Pedagogy of the Oppressed* (2000). For Kendra, school was what it was; how could it be otherwise? She did not see the point of thinking about school—or writing, for that matter. These were simply things one did when told, according to specifications laid out by others.

Fortunately, Kendra's story is not an altogether unhappy one. Many students internalize the labels that institutions place on them—remedial, basic, unprepared—and live down to them, as it were. But perhaps owing to her success in high school, her inner strength, or Amy's persistence (or some combination of these), Kendra began to blossom. Her motivation and her performance improved. Why? Because she began the long process of claiming her education and coming to see that her ideas and her writing could matter. This process started when Kendra acknowledged that her experiences in school (and elsewhere, for that matter) were not natural or inevitable, but instead were the result of choices that people—including herself, but mostly others—had made. This recognition helped Kendra explore why she felt alienated from her own education and why she so often felt she had nothing to say in her classes. And slowly, as she learned to use the reflective tools that Amy provided in class, Kendra began to learn how *not* to take for granted her experiences and her received ideas about how the world works and to see new possibilities. In short, she was learning to become a reflective thinker.

In *How We Think* (1933), John Dewey claims that without the capacity for reflective thinking, we become slaves to imitation, tradition, and instruction. In other words, we will do what we see others doing, what has always been done, or what we are told to do, without considering whether other possibilities exist. Reflective thinking allows us to formulate meaningful questions; identify, interpret, and analyze information; sniff out biases and assumptions; recognize the limitations of our own worldview and empathize with those of others; and marshal various kinds of evidence to support our stances. Some people call these the characteristics of "academic" discourse; we think that in a deliberative democracy, they should be understood as the right and responsibility of every citizen.

This includes teachers. As teachers, we need to step back from our practice and consider carefully how and why we are doing what we are doing. And like Kendra, we benefit from identifying and questioning the "scripts" that others hand us. As Joy Ritchie and David Wilson (2000) explain in their book *Teacher Narrative as Critical Inquiry*, we are surrounded by cultural, institutional, and personal "scripts" that frame the way we see things—including ourselves. These scripts emerge, for example, when we ask teachers to complete a "scenes of teaching" activity that mimics the "scenes of writing" activity Kendra had such a hard time completing in Amy's class. That old, stern Gradgrind makes an appearance. Our wonderfully kind, perpetually smiling first-grade teacher takes shape. The self-sacrificing, ever-dependable, invariably even-keeled Superteacher pops up. What emerges in these moments is a recognition that our sense of ourselves as teachers (just like Kendra's sense of self as a student and writer) is never natural or inevitable; it is always "storied"—and therefore potentially "re-storied."

> In order to re-story our teaching lives, we must first discover/uncover the scripts we have been handed.

But in order to re-story our teaching lives, we must first discover/uncover the scripts we have been handed.

Reading Our Scripts

Rules of Teaching

Take a moment and quickly list all the "rules of teaching" you have learned over the years. These might include: "Lay down the law early." "Never let them see you sweat." "Always write the day's lesson on the board at the beginning of class." "Never use red pen." "Begin where they are." "Make learning fun." Jot down the ideas as they come to you. ❖

This activity helps us call to conscious awareness ideas about teaching that may be only half-articulated or that we have come to take for granted. But in reflecting on these rules, the trick is *not* to take them for granted, but instead to ask ourselves: Are these rules useful? Do they make teaching easier? Do I agree with all of them? Do I ever break them in my own teaching? Have I seen others break them, and with what consequences? How and why was I taught these rules? Or did I learn them without direct instruction? The point is to explore our own values, beliefs, and assumptions about teaching in order to clarify them, by way of either justification or alteration.

What most teachers find when they take the time to reflect on the "rules" they live by as teachers is that none (or almost none) of the rules is hard and fast. Most of us can think of times when, for one reason or another, we broke one of our own rules. Maybe a particular class needed to see us get mad before they would respond. Maybe a particular student needed to stop thinking that learning could always be fun and just had to buckle down and do the work. Maybe we couldn't immediately answer a question on the spot. In any case, the "rules" we live by as teachers most often turn out not to be rules at all, but rather general guidelines that *usually*, but not always, serve us well. But because teaching is messy, unpredictable work that involves messy, unpredictable human beings, we cannot rely on strict recipes or blueprints for teaching. A good part of the work will always be more art than science.

> We cannot rely on strict recipes or blueprints for teaching. A good part of the work will always be more art than science.

And so it is with writing. We ask our students to do a similar activity that probes their understanding of the "rules of writing" (see Activity 3-1).

Typically, students' lists of writing rules include proscriptions and prescriptions such as "Never split infinitives," "Avoid sentence fragments," "Always have a clear 'thesis statement' in your introduction," and "Conclusions should restate the thesis statement in different words." But as we discuss these rules in our classes, students are

Activity 3-1
Rules of Writing

In your notebook, list all the rules of "good writing" you have learned over the years. This could include rules such as "Never use *I*," "Always use active voice," and "Never end a sentence with a preposition."

After you complete your list, step back from it and ask yourself: Are these rules useful? Do they make writing easier? Do any of them give me trouble? Why? Do I ever break them in my own writing? Have I seen others break them? What happens when these rules are broken? What are the consequences of breaking/bending certain rules? Do some carry heavier "penalties" than others? Write for a few minutes on the questions that strike you as most interesting.

Teaching Writing That Matters © 2008 by Chris W. Gallagher and Amy Lee, Scholastic Professional.

quick to point out that published, renowned writers break these rules with startling regularity. Authors of children's books use incomplete sentences to build suspense: "Then he heard a sound. A scary sound." The producers of a famous television series famously split an infinitive: "To boldly go where no man has gone before." Revered writers offer up several-page run-on sentences in their classics. (Faulkner, anyone?) The list goes on and on. (Sometimes, we ask students to collect and bring to class examples of "good writing" that break the rules they have identified so as to discuss and analyze the effect; it is never difficult to find such examples.)

But wait, you might say, don't we need to know the rules before we break them? Well, as commonsensical as that old adage sounds, studies have found that readers often do not recognize "errors" in the work of published writing, but will recognize those same "errors"—and berate their creators—in student writing (Williams, 1981). Readers don't identify "errors" in published texts because they assume intention: it may *look* like an error, but surely the published writer was going for effect. Meanwhile, readers do identify errors in student texts because they assume students don't know the rules and have transgressed unintentionally. What this means is that "errors" are rhetorical; that is, they are a matter of the writer's authority and purpose, the readers' expectations, and the context in which the piece is written and read. And so maybe our old chestnut needs to be revised to read, "You must convince your readers that you know the rules before you break them." Or at least there must be a payoff to the rule-breaking—it needs to get us somewhere.

The upshot of all this is not that we should ignore "the rules" or teach students that they don't matter. We're not proposing a new rule to "always break rules." Rules exist for a reason. They represent certain *values*: "Never use *I*" is based on the value of objectivity or authorial detachment; "Always use transitions" is based on the value of linear reasoning. But these values are neither universal nor handled the same way in contexts where they do hold sway. For example, in some academic disciplines, using *I* is forbidden, but other disciplines value a strong sense of authorial presence and invest-ment in the argument and research and thus deem *I* appropriate, even essential. Similarly, William Faulkner's labyrinthine sentences in "The Bear" would not do for a job letter, just as the conventional prose of a job letter would not be an appropriate vehicle for telling a hunting story.

Undoubtedly, it would be much easier if we could simply learn, once and for all, the rules for "good writing" and "good teaching." Then, as long as we colored inside the lines, we would be "successful." But neither of these activities can be reduced to algorithms and prescriptions. Even so-called best practices are never foolproof or equally appropriate to all teaching or writing contexts. That is why we don't present the Seven Habits of Highly Effective Teachers or the Nine Keys to Unlocking Your Writing Potential. Good writing and teaching are not the result of conforming to some universal ideal or following some lockstep formula; they are the result of writers and teachers engaging in reflective practice so as to make smart, informed choices among the options available to them in a given situation.

When we do engage in this kind of reflective thinking, we not only become more thoughtful about the scripts we're handed, but we also uncover/discover our own scripts: our often latent and half-formed but nonetheless consequential beliefs.

Teaching Writing That Matters

Rewriting Our Scripts

"This I Believe About Teaching"
What are your core beliefs about teaching? What key values shape your teaching life? How did you arrive at these beliefs and values? Can you think of an event or inter-action that led you to these beliefs and values? Write a brief (approximately 500-word) essay that explores two or three beliefs and/or values that you hold most dear as a teacher. Title it "This I Believe About Teaching." ❖

This activity is a shameless rip-off of a shameless rip-off. National Public Radio's *This I Believe* essay series is a revival of a popular 1950s radio show of the same name by Edward R. Murrow. Both shows solicit audio essays (another form you could use for this activity), though NPR accepts written essays online. The idea is simple: to encourage "ordinary people" to share the personal beliefs and values that shape their lives. The purpose of this sharing is to create a public dialogue, an exchange about what is most important to us as human beings.

Our purposes here are the same, though they revolve around what is most impor-tant to us as *teachers*. The short length of the essay requires us to identify and articulate only our most important beliefs and values. In our experience, the sharing of these short essays among teachers never fails to solicit engaging conversation. And no won-der: this project brings us right to the heart of why we do what we do.

Just as we benefit from articulating and discussing our beliefs and values about teaching, writers benefit from doing the same about writing. This is why so many cre-ative writers develop statements of their "poetics," or what is most important to them as writers. We believe it is especially important for adolescent writers to do this work—precisely because so few of them see themselves as writers. If they are asked to *become* writers—as they are in Writing Studies classrooms—then students will need to wrestle with the identity of a writer. This means they will need opportunities to explore their experiences, beliefs, and values about writing—positive or negative.

Not surprisingly, we have found students less prepared to claim their values and beliefs about writing than teachers are about teaching. But informal, idea-generating activities can help students see that in fact, they have a wealth of writing experiences. Once those experiences are excavated, the task is to draw insights from them.

Our answer to the conundrum of students' having a wealth of experience but being reluctant to claim those experiences is, perhaps ironically, to push them hard to make some strong claims, as described in Activity 3-2.

This activity does a number of things at once: it helps students reflect on and capture their experiences; it allows them to air their concerns about writing and about

---

Activity 3-2

Two or Three Things I Know for Sure About Writing

In her memoir *Two or Three Things I Know for Sure*, Dorothy Allison (1996) uses the phrase in her title to frame some of the most important ideas in the book. For example, she writes, "Two or three things I know for sure, and one is that I'd rather go naked than wear the coat the world has made for me" (71).

Interestingly, Allison's book is largely about what she doesn't know: what confuses her. But statements like this one are her attempt to salvage some clarity from the jumble; through writing, she is trying to figure out what she really does know "for sure."

For this 500-word essay about writing, borrow Allison's format. What are two or three things you know for sure about writing? These could be things you know about the act of writing (it's painful, takes a long time, relieves tension, is a necessary evil) or things you know about yourself as a writer (you hate writing, love writing, are a good creative writer but are terrified by all other kinds of writing). Whatever you choose to write about, explain as best you can how you came to know these things. In other words, tell a story, with appropriate details, that shows how you learned what you now know about writing.

Don't worry if after writing about the "things you know," you're not so sure anymore. That's exactly what happens to Allison, and all writers, sometimes.

Teaching Writing That Matters © 2008 by Chris W. Gallagher and Amy Lee, Scholastic Professional.

Teaching Writing That Matters

themselves as writers (this often makes for terrific classroom conversation); it helps them claim their knowledge about writing and themselves as writers; and it gives them practice writing short essays. Even when the claims they make in these essays are largely negative—as they often are—there is something empowering about "owning" the claim. Also, as the prompt suggests, the act of claiming often precipitates rethinking; sometimes when we are forced to claim a belief in writing, rather than allowing it to remain tacit and half-formed, we realize that we cannot stand by it.

Helping students conduct this kind of self-inventory and self-assessment—and doing so ourselves as teachers—is a crucial step in teaching (and learning) the art of reflective thinking. But it is only the beginning. It is one thing to identify our guiding beliefs, another to reshape them, and yet another to *use* them to guide our work. In order to do the latter, we must look back at our past and into our present, but also forward to our future. Like Kendra, we need to find ways to use reflective thinking to control the course of our lives and our work. One simple way to begin doing this is to set goals with our beliefs in mind.

Acting Out Our Own Scripts

Teaching Goals

With your beliefs about teaching in mind, list a set of goals you have for your teaching of writing. (Examples: I want to learn new strategies for responding to student work. I want to try using student writing portfolios. I want students to be more reflective about the choices they make as writers. I want my students to write for public audiences.)

For each goal, explain why *it's important to you. What belief does it help you act on? Is this goal an end in itself, or does it lead to other consequences?*

Also for each goal, consider how you will know whether you've achieved it. Is the consequence observable? Can you chart your progress toward it? ❖

You might notice that the questions in this activity aren't all that different from the questions often posed under the heading of "outcomes assessment." Typically, for outcomes assessment, we ask, "What should students know and be able to do? How will we measure those outcomes? What will we do with the data we collect?" Our questions might also evoke for you the idea of "backward design," in which teachers are asked to consider first the ideal outcomes of their teaching, and then design learning activities, instructional strategies, and assessment measures that will bring about and document those outcomes. Our questions might even smack of "strategic planning" more generally. All these processes begin with the articulation of outcomes and then have us consider how to achieve those outcomes.

We find value in some of this work, and we have used some of these ideas and approaches ourselves. (Wiggins & McTighe, 2005, and Fink, 2003, are particularly useful.) We resist the term *outcomes*, though, both because it is too simplistic (teaching and learning are too messy to predict or manage the way this linear language suggests) and because it is misleading (it makes education sound terminal, rather than ongoing). As you know, we are interested in ensuring that teaching and learning are consequential; but that is different from saying they should have "outcomes." Of course they have outcomes; all human activity does. But some outcomes—and we know this, alas, from experience—don't matter at all, either to teachers or to students.

Besides, and perhaps more importantly, we are concerned with what comes *before*, what informs the identification of outcomes—or, as we prefer, consequences. For us, the important part of this activity is the tying of our goals to our beliefs. While we do think it's important to think about how we'll know if we've met our goals, we think it's equally important to clarify, at least for ourselves, the rationales for these goals in the first place. We think of goal-setting as a connective activity for reflective practitioners: It ties together our beliefs and our practices. It grounds us in an ongoing process whose most important "outcome" is reflective practice itself.

And so it is with young writers, for whom the setting of goals is likely to be an unusual and even sometimes uncomfortable experience. We ask students to identify their goals early on in our courses, after some reflective activities designed to help them articulate their beliefs. In addition to setting them on a path of reflective practice, this

Activity 3-3
Writing Goals

1. With your reflective writing about your beliefs about writing in mind, brainstorm a list of five to ten goals you have for your writing. (Examples: I want to use my writing time more wisely. I want to express my good ideas more clearly. I want to learn more about what kinds of writing I'm good and not so good at.)

2. For each goal, explain why it's important to you. If you do achieve it, what will it "get" you? What will it allow you to do or to know?

3. Also for each goal, write about how you will know if you've achieved it. How can you chart your own progress toward your goals?

Teaching Writing That Matters © 2008 by Chris W. Gallagher and Amy Lee, Scholastic Professional.

activity also serves as an informal assessment moment for us: we learn a great deal about students by the goals they set for themselves. As a result, we can make our courses more responsive to our students. Then, throughout the semester, we ask students to return to their goals often in order to gauge their progress on them—or to adjust, drop, or add goals. Activity 3-3 is a simple template for early-semester goal setting.

Too rarely are adolescents asked to set their own goals for learning or writing (or life). Too rarely are they provided an opportunity to connect their beliefs with their practices, acting out their own scripts. As Kendra's story shows us, adolescents too often move through the world at someone else's direction, reading from others' scripts. But if we want our students to become writers, as Writing Studies proposes, it is important to help them write and act out their own scripts. In this way, their writing will come to matter to them—making it all the more likely that their writing will matter to others as well.

> **If we want our students to become writers, it is important to help them write and act out their own scripts.**

Chapter 4

Rhetorical Awareness in Teaching and Writing

Meet Cady, Chris's daughter:

> *A big day at school: the eighth-grade state writing test was today. For a girl who professes to "hate hate hate tests," she's positively glowing. What gives?*
>
> *"I aced it," she announces to no one in particular at the dinner table.*
>
> *Aced it?*
>
> *"It was 'descriptive writing.' We were supposed to describe an object that is important to us. I knew most of the kids would write about their iPods and things like that. So I wrote about my photo album. We've been doing these sensory exercises, so I wrote about what it looks like, how it feels, blah blah blah. But then"—she pauses for dramatic effect—"I wrote about how it holds precious memories"—rolls her eyes—"and about how we sit down as a family"—pretends to stick her finger down her throat and makes gagging sounds—"and make new memories by talking about the experiences we've shared. It was a beautiful thing."*
>
> *In case we missed her meaning: "Because, you know, my English teacher said teachers score the tests, and teachers eat that sentimental stuff up."*

Cady's prediction held up: she "aced" the test. What should we make of this? That she "beat the system"? That the test more or less required her to be someone she wasn't in order to succeed? That it solicited and rewarded dishonesty and pandering?

Maybe so. Part of us is saddened by this story. Surely Cady's—and her teacher's, and those teacher-scorers'—time and thought could be better spent. On the other hand, our writers' hearts are gladdened to see a fellow writer "reading" the situation and making motivated choices about how to negotiate it. Clearly, Cady has a repertoire of writing strategies at her disposal, and she has the confidence and the competence to use those strategies effectively, for her own purposes as well as others'.

Unfortunately, however, many adolescent writers are less like Cady than like Michelle (Chapter 1) or Kendra (Chapter 3). They haven't had the opportunity to develop the reflective habits of mind required to become agile writers. Unlike Cady, they are not rhetorically aware; that is, they don't write with their purposes, audiences, and contexts in mind.

In fact, even many college students (certainly not all) struggle to be rhetorically aware. We regularly have students in our classes who were served quite well by the five-paragraph essay form that remains a staple in many high school classrooms (largely owing to testing requirements, as we discuss in Chapter 2), but who struggle in college.

For example, Amy recently worked with a student, John, who resisted moving away from formulaic writing because he had been rewarded for his mastery of it in high school. But John clearly had hit a wall: his 5- to 7-page college essays consisted of five 1- to $1\frac{1}{2}$-page paragraphs! In addition to running into organization problems, John found himself hamstrung as he tried to think through complex ideas.

What John needed, then, was not a way to write shorter paragraphs, but new ways of framing his thoughts—in fact, new ways of thinking. And in order to achieve this, he needed to let go of the idea that he had at his command a universally serviceable, one-size-fits-all form of academic writing.

Similarly, students sometimes become accomplished in a particular kind of writing and then attempt, unsuccessfully, to transport that way of writing into different writing situations. For example, like John, Michael was identified as a strong writer in high school. In high school, he graduated from a pre-STEM (science, technology, engineering, math) career preparation track, and his understanding of writing was governed by the conventions of scientific writing. He could not understand why he was struggling in Amy's literature course. He could not understand why his approach—characterized by short paragraphs, unequivocal statements of results and findings, and a detached authorial stance—wasn't cutting it in his literary analyses. He couldn't understand why providing a passage from a poem to support his thesis, without interpreting the passage, was not enough.

The problem—as Amy and Michael discussed each week in her office for ten weeks in a row—was not that Michael couldn't write; it was that, like Michelle in Chapter 1, he was writing in only one way. He was good at writing scientific analyses, but he was not able to bring his interpretive, organizational, reasoning, or argumentative skills—which are equally important in both instances—to bear on literary analyses. He was at once a proficient and a novice writer. In order to become an agile writer, he had to learn to use what he knew in multiple writing situations. This was not a lesson easily learned.

We see a parallel among teachers. Perhaps because human nature longs for certainty and predictability, we teachers often seek out activities, projects, assignments, strategies, and lessons that are "foolproof." We want all our students to succeed, and so naturally, we want classroom practices that will serve all students equally well. Meanwhile, policymakers and administrators, concerned with "quality assurance," often push for standardized curriculum and instruction. They want the universally serviceable, one-size-fits-all equivalent of the five-paragraph essay. No wonder so many books written for educators these days reveal the Nine Strategies to Unlock Students' Potential or the Seven Rules of Assessment or the Five Key Curriculum Principles. (By the way, why do these formulations always involve odd numbers?)

To be sure, some teaching practices are better than others, just as some writing practices are better than others. We would favor respectful interactions with students over berating them almost every time, and we can think of few circumstances in which we would encourage writers to make sure they didn't know anything about their topic. But identifying generally effective and generally ineffective practices is not the same thing as attempting to create an all-purpose formula for teaching or writing. As we hope the "Rules " exercises in Chapter 3 suggest, there is a large gap between general guidelines that serve us well and hard-and-fast rules to which we offer our blind obedience.

The point is that writing and teaching require rhetorical awareness—an ability to size up a situation, assess what it requires of us, and respond accordingly. Different purposes and audiences call for different strategies. "Best practices" may offer good ideas, but active intelligence and sound judgment should drive our work.

Fortunately, we and our students already have a great deal of rhetorical awareness; the trick is to bring it to the surface and to learn how to deploy it, as Cady is able to do in our opening vignette.

> "Best practices" may offer good ideas, but active intelligence and sound judgment should drive our work.

Tapping Rhetorical Awareness

Class Scripts

It is midsemester and three of your classes, though similar in content, are playing out completely differently. One is high-energy and high-ability but is having trouble focusing on the work. Another is just the opposite: low-energy, struggling, but earnest. A third is a mix of these—the students are extremely heterogeneous. For reasons you can't quite explain, none of the classes is going as well as you'd like; although some students are doing good work (and others aren't), you feel disconnected from each group and fear that you and they are starting to go through the motions. In hopes of turning things around, you want to address each group directly, sharing your sense of how things are going and inviting them to troubleshoot with you.

What will you say to each class? Write a short script for each class. ❖

Each course we teach is a potent, unique mix of individuals. Even when we teach the same course back-to-back, vast differences emerge in attitudes, opinions, values, performance, and so on. Activities that hit the mark in our second-period class will bomb third period. Students in fourth period ace the assessment, but the students in sixth, who received the same instruction, fail miserably. And then of course there are the irreducibly complex individuals *within* each class. It's dizzying, mind-boggling.

Like the other activities in this book, this one is intended to bring to the surface latent skills and abilities that most of us already have, but that we don't spend much time thinking about or honing. Teachers rarely find this activity difficult. But consider what we must do to complete it: assess not only *what* is going on but *why*; identify a proper intervention; articulate that intervention; and invite students to undertake it with us. And not only that: we need to do that across three different sets of circumstances. Our thinking needs to be flexible and creative. To be sure, we might call upon some of our old reliable strategies. We might use the "sandwich" response model (praise-critique-praise) in each case, for example. But *how* we do this, and the content of the response itself, will vary, depending on the unique circumstances presented in each classroom.

This is why a toolbox, or a bag of tricks, is never enough. After all, a builder who doesn't know how to use the tools at her disposal, or how to decide which tool might best suit a particular job, wouldn't be much of a builder. A builder needs to be able to match tools to her purposes. At times, she may need to put tools to new uses, bend her existing tools to fit new needs, or fashion new tools.

This applies to writers as well as teachers. We can give writers activities, exercises, strategies, and skills. We can teach them how to punctuate, spell, or use a graphic organizer. But unless writers know how to *use* these tools across the dizzying array of writing situations they will face in school and beyond it—well, then, we've not taught them to write with rhetorical awareness.

Again, the trick is to call to the surface what adolescent writers know on an unconscious level. It's certainly the case that adolescents know how to *speak* differently to different people when their purposes differ. The problem is that they "forget" this—or, to be fair, rarely have occasion to remember it—when it comes to school writing.

There are numerous ways to tap into students' latent rhetorical awareness. In our college classes, we sometimes ask our students to complete an activity in which they are to imagine that they've decided not to return to school the next semester. They need to write short letters to (1) a parent, grandparent, or other adult relative, (2) their best friend, and (3) a school official. This activity quickly surfaces the rhetorical awareness our students already have. Even letters that are written quickly demonstrate thoughtful deliberation and rhetorical savvy. The letters to family members, for example, tend not to announce the decision right away, but instead gingerly broach the subject after some preparation (which often involves buttering up the reader). However, when writing to friends, writers usually open with the decision, assuming an existing conversation on the topic, and then discuss their feelings about or the ramifications of the decision. In these letters, differences in diction, tone, and voice are stark, often beginning with the salutation. Every time we read them, we are struck by the wealth of knowledge students have about purpose and audience and the array of strategies they have at their disposal. We are also struck by how rarely students call on these strategies in the course of their writing lives.

We are mindful that the example in the preceding paragraph reflects *our* rhetorical context: the struggle to decide whether to stay in college is a powerful topic for our "audience" of first-year college students, who are in the midst of a major life transition and who need opportunities to think through, record, and openly investigate this experience. In fact, it's not uncommon for students to want to dwell a bit on this exercise and their responses, or for them to point to this moment twelve weeks later in the final course evaluations as one of the most powerful moments for them in the class.

This activity is effective because it combines a topic that is meaningful and immediate for students with explicit attention to *how* writers handle it. Activity 4-1 uses the same basic idea, but a simpler template.

Completing this activity helps students understand that their purpose and audience shape everything about their texts, from the genre conventions they use to the details they choose to disclose to the sequencing of information to the tone and diction they use.

This simple exercise can lead students to a more

> Understanding how purpose, audience, and context shape writing (in other words, developing rhetorical awareness) is a matter of asking certain kinds of questions about the texts we read and write.

Activity 4-1
Three of Me

Write three different 200-word descriptions of yourself:

1. to introduce yourself to the rest of the class,
2. for the school yearbook, and
3. for a MySpace page.

Teaching Writing That Matters © 2008 by Chris W. Gallagher and Amy Lee, Scholastic Professional.

sophisticated and extensive investigation of the importance of rhetorical context. In large part, understanding how purpose, audience, and context shape writing (in other words, developing rhetorical awareness) is a matter of asking certain kinds of questions about the texts we read and write. We can practice asking those questions about the texts that we write for our students.

Conducting Rhetorical Analysis

The Rhetoric of Classroom Texts

Choose a classroom text that you have written for students—an assignment, a set of instructions, a course guide, a narrative comment on a student paper, and so on. (Alternatively, you could choose other kinds of school texts: a curriculum scope and sequence, a set of state standards, district objectives, school improvement goals.) Reading it carefully, perhaps multiple times, ask yourself the following questions:

PURPOSE: *What is this text intended to do? Are its goals implicit or explicit?*

AUDIENCE: *To whom is the text addressed? Is the audience addressed directly, or is it implied? Does the text demonstrate that the writer is audience-aware? Does he or she invoke shared assumptions or beliefs? Are other viewpoints, including possible objec-*

tions, represented and confronted? What writerly choices (in voice, diction, tone, content) clue us in to the intended audience?

STRATEGIES: *How does the writer position herself or himself and the text in relation to readers? What "moves" does the writer make? (For instance, does the writer use rhetorical questions, humor, or self-deprecation?)*

FORM: *What genre is this text? What conventions of the genre do you see? (For example, how long is it? Does it have a title? Are the paragraphs long or short? Is the language simple or complex? Does it use any specialized or "insider" language? How is it organized? Are there any headings? What kinds of transitions? Is there any "signposting" ["First, we will . . . ; then we will . . ."]?) Are there places where the text departs from genre conventions? If so, was this a conscious choice by the writer, and if so, why do you think he or she made that choice?*

SITUATIONAL FACTORS: *What else in the writing situation informs what this text says, or how it says it? How does the medium affect the message? Was the writer helped or hindered by available technologies? Do any recent events cast a particular light (or shadow) on the text?* ❖

We encourage you to analyze your own classroom texts—to *study* them as *writing*—because the activity forces you to get outside your intentions and see what's really on the page (to the extent that this is possible). Often, doing so leads us to revise our texts. Because it helps us see how our teaching texts work, rather than just how we desire them to work, rhetorical analysis is a way to make visible to ourselves the results of the choices we have made and point us toward alternative choices we might make.

We want writers in our classrooms to gain a similar appreciation for the array of choices available to them and to assess the consequences of their choices. But students often find rhetorical analysis to be unfamiliar, unnatural, and even uncomfortable. Often trained only to read for content and to approach texts as containers for information, rather than the dynamic social acts that they are, students are generally more comfortable exploring *what* texts mean than examining *how* they mean. This is especially true of published texts; students generally do not consider the ways in which "professional" writing is shaped by its rhetorical contexts and results from the choices that real writers make.

Reading rhetorically—conducting rhetorical analysis—is important in Writing Studies classrooms because all texts become an opportunity for students to explore the world of ideas as well as to develop their rhetorical awareness. To help students read rhetorically, we can guide them to study both how texts work (how they're put together) and the work that they do (how they act on the world). We can help students get inside texts, reading them from the inside out, as it were. In doing so, we do not ignore the content of texts, of course, but we add an emphasis on composition, paying particular attention to *how* and *why* texts are put together in the ways they are. This helps students become more thoughtful, engaged, and effective readers and writers.

> **All texts become an opportunity for students to explore the world of ideas as well as to develop their rhetorical awareness.**

But, you might be thinking, how is all this going to help my students master the research paper, the thesis-driven essay, or the lab report? Wouldn't it be more efficient to teach them the conventions of these genres directly? True, we might get students to approximate these forms with enough explicit instruction in conventions (including, perhaps, penalties for transgressions against them). However, we do writers a much better service by helping them cultivate rhetorical awareness, including the ability to analyze genres and rhetorical situations for themselves. Even if our goal is to have students learn these traditional genres, our experience has been that they do so much more readily, and enthusiastically, when they are able to understand *how* and *why* these genres work, and how and why they're different from other genres.

Rhetorical analysis is applicable to all texts, but because students are generally unaccustomed to this kind of work, we often begin with the familiar texts of advertising. (A more general rhetorical analysis activity is presented in Chapter 7, "Project Toolbox 2.") Advertising is readily available and typically far from subtle. Also, through this work, students develop critical, skeptical habits of mind as they read and view this pervasive and sometimes pernicious world of discourse.

Activity 4-2
The Rhetoric of Advertising

Find a copy of three magazines with very different audiences—say, *Fine Cooking, Popular Mechanics,* and *Seventeen.* First, thumb through each issue, paying particular attention to the advertisements in each. Then do the following:

1. List the products in the ads in each magazine.
2. Identify the key features of the ads on each list. Consider the following:
   - the kind of product (for example, personal hygiene, clothing, auto parts, kitchenware)
   - the size of the ads
   - the color schemes
   - the visual depiction of the product
   - who, if anyone, is using the product in the ad (gender, race, other physical characteristics)
   - other visual material in the ad
   - the words, if any, used in the ad (including font and number of words)
   - the tone of the ad (is it jokey? serious? fun?)
   - the information presented about the product
3. Now you have three lists of ads and their key characteristics. For each list, ask yourself these questions:
   - Why would the ads have these characteristics?
   - Based on this list of characteristics, what can I infer about the target audience of each magazine?
   - Can I learn anything about the assumed values, beliefs, needs, wants, or characteristics of this audience from analyzing the ads?
4. Compare the lists and identify overlaps and differences.

Teaching Writing That Matters © 2008 by Chris W. Gallagher and Amy Lee, Scholastic Professional.

Activity 4-2 asks students to study texts in order to reach conclusions about their (differing) rhetorical contexts: *whom* they are intended for, *what* they are intended to do, and *how* they attempt to do that work. (You could also use television ads, asking students to keep an observation log on ads during three different types of programming, such as a football game, a soap opera, and a children's cartoon.) After engaging students in discussion about their conclusions, you might ask each student or group to write an ad for a product of their choice, targeting a particular audience by placing it in a particular magazine or on a particular television show. You could also extend the rhetorical analysis by asking students to revise an ad with the aim of making it effective in an alternative rhetorical context—a different magazine or show.

Rhetorical analysis is a powerful tool because it makes visible the choices that writers make. It helps students understand that texts are not natural or inevitable; they are the result of decisions made by writers who (one hopes) are thinking hard about their purposes and audiences.

> Writers always could have made other choices; texts could always be other than what they are; revision is always possible.

Implied in all this (but easy to forget) are some simple truths: writers always could have made other choices; texts could always be other than what they are; revision is always possible. This notion of revision is important to the Writing Studies classroom.

The Art of Re-Vision

Re-Visioning Classroom Texts
Take one of the classroom texts you've analyzed and change it in some radical way. For example, consider changing:

- **POINT OF VIEW:** *What if you rewrote that comment on the student's argument essay as if you were his opponent, rather than his teacher? What if you* *rewrote that short story assignment as though you were an editor soliciting manuscripts?*

- **GENRE:** *What if you rewrote your course guide (syllabus) as a letter to students? What if you rewrote that set of project criteria as a list of questions students can ask themselves?*
- **AUDIENCE:** *What if you rewrote your response to that student's story as though you were reviewing it for publication? What if you rewrote that proposal assignment as a professional Call for Proposals?* ❖

In our experience, here's what happens when teachers try this activity. First, they tell us we're crazy, that these examples are strange and awkward. But then, as they spend some time trying out the activity, they begin to generate all kinds of new ideas about how to communicate with their students. They begin to see that the discursive world of the classroom is largely taken for granted; the genres and their conventions are so familiar as to have become nearly invisible. If nothing else, this re-vision activity gives us a bit of critical distance from kinds of writing we do every day.

Because teaching is such a messy and complex practice—more art than science, as we have argued—it's important to remember that it is as much about *re*vision as about vision. Following poet Adrienne Rich (2001b), we think of "revision" as seeing again, or entering an old text (or script, or map, or road, or course, or classroom, or activity) from a new direction (p. 11). As teachers, this ability to step back from our usual practices or unexamined assumptions and expectations keeps us honest. In the words of writing teacher Nancy Welch (1997), we need to "get restless" with our teaching, asking ourselves, "Something missing, something else?" (p. 136).

Adolescent writers often have a difficult time understanding revision as "seeing again"; instead, they tend to conflate it with editing, or even proofreading: getting the words right, rather than developing the ideas. To help students re-vision their own writing, we can ask them to do the same sort of work we do in Activity 4-3 with their first drafts of any project.

For reflective practitioners, ultimately all teaching and all writing is re-vision; we are constantly looking, and looking again, at our practice. We deliberately slow down the

Activity 4-3
Re-Visioning Possibilities

Let's push ourselves to practice a new level of revision with these drafts of our current project. Remember that revision is not only about making drafts "better"; it's also about seeing alternatives—new possibilities for our writing. Consider the following possibilities:

1. Change the *point of view* of the text. For example, if you have written a first-person personal essay, what would it look like from the perspective of someone else in the story? If you have written an argument essay, what would it look like from your opponent's point of view?

2. Change the *genre (form)* of the text. For example, rewrite your essay as a short story. Or rewrite your argument essay as an editorial for the local newspaper or a letter to a family member or a brochure for an organization supporting or opposing the cause you've written about.

3. Change the *audience* of the text. For example, if your personal essay has a general audience, rewrite it for your family. If your argument essay has an academic audience, rewrite it for your peers, or your family, or a public official.

Teaching Writing That Matters © 2008 by Chris W. Gallagher and Amy Lee, Scholastic Professional.

process, consider our options, and choose wisely from among them based on our assessment of the situation at hand. In this age of fast teaching and fast writing, it's easy to settle for "good enough," for what's generally serviceable. But if we want our students to become writers, if we want to help them write in ways that matter to them and to others, we need to help them explore what Rich (2001a) calls "the arts of the possible" (p. 146). We need to help them get restless, be agile, and develop rhetorical awareness.

Chapter 5

Community in Teaching and Writing

Meet Joe:

For the first time ever, Joe's getting bad grades. He can't seem to settle down and do the work. The transition to high school has been tough. Many of his middle school friends are attending other high schools in the city. The few friends who are in this school have splintered off into separate groups. He doesn't know where he belongs. He's spent the whole first quarter in a fog, going through the motions, mostly just trying to get through the day.

Second semester, Joe enrolls in debate class. He went to a summer debate camp, and that was fun. Besides, the "debate kids," as everyone calls them, seem interesting. The debate coach's room is different from the other teachers' rooms. Music is often playing; the kids sit around talking or doing research at computers; the coach roams around, helping whomever seems to need it. Joe likes the laid-back atmosphere.

The first day of debate class, Joe walks into a heated argument in progress. Several kids sit around a table arguing about stem cell research. Joe's never seen or heard this kind of excitement in his school—not about schoolwork, anyway. One kid's been scribbling away at the table. He looks up at Joe and says, "Hey, new guy. I'm trying to write my aff case. Those kids at North are going to destroy me if I don't get this worked out. I'm thinking of running justice as my criterion. Let me run this by you; tell me what you think."

Joe quickly slides into an open seat. He has no idea what this kid is talking about. But he knows he belongs here.

Joe went on to perform exceedingly well at novice debate tournaments. He spent long hours working on his cases. At the same time, his performance in other classes improved. Why? Joe's story reminds us that in order to feel we *have* something to say, we need someone who cares what we have to say.

> In order to feel we *have* something to say, we need someone who cares what we have to say.

This is a key tenet of Writing Studies classrooms, in which students write for real purposes and audiences and study how writing actually works in the world. Students are not writing only to be evaluated, merely because they *have* to say something. And they're not studying language in the abstract, out of context. They are writing and reading with authentic purposes and audiences in mind, entering into meaningful conversations with others, just as Joe is learning to do at his debate tournaments.

As we noted in Chapter 2, this kind of classroom is not easy to build in this age of test-'em-till-they-drop, which places so much emphasis on measuring individual competence on isolated, usually inauthentic writing tasks. But as we have emphasized throughout this book, writing is an irreducibly social and rhetorical act; we cannot hope to understand it—much less help our students excel at it—unless and until we conceive of how it works in actual communities.

And so it's important to think about our classrooms as communities—places where our common interests require us to work on and work out problems, issues, and shared concerns. Classrooms can feel like profoundly inauthentic social spaces—but they need not. As John Dewey (1966/1916) famously argued in *Democracy and Education*, schools and classrooms are not merely practice or preparation for engaging in social life; they *are* social life. They are themselves communities, and they are located within communities: neighborhoods, towns and cities, states, the nation, the world.

Teaching Writing That Matters

For Dewey, one of the primary purposes of schooling is to help students learn to live well together—in other words, to find and create community with other human beings. He notes the importance of communication in this endeavor: "Not only is social life identical with communication, but all communication (and hence all genuine social life) is educative. To have received communication is to have an

> **Students can and should write in and into the classroom community, but also in and into communities beyond it.**

enlarged and changed experience" (1966/1916, p. 5). This is an important idea, but we would expand it a bit: to have *participated in* communication, whether as a sender or a receiver, is to have had an enlarged and changed experience. And enlarged and changed experiences, as Dewey rightly suggests elsewhere in *Democracy and Education*, are the whole point of education (p. 76).

What all this means for Writing Studies classrooms is this: Students can and should write in and into the classroom community, but also in and into communities beyond it. Think of Joe: he immediately recognizes—and is excited by—a classroom community where writing is valued, and that makes all the difference. In turn, this community leads him to write into the larger debate community across his state.

Similarly, Cady (Chapter 4) was not just trying to *write to* teachers who would read her test; she was attempting to *write into* the teaching community. And she did so by upholding their standards and invoking their values. She understood a key tenet of Writing Studies: that rhetorical contexts are shaped by communities of people who make choices about what they will and will not value in writing. This is true of all rhetorical contexts, whether we're talking about a classroom, an academic discipline, a school, a business office, a faith group, a political body, or the blogosphere. Each of the communities governing these contexts has its own, ever-evolving set of standards and values, and these translate into expectations for writing. These expectations, and the standards and values, may be implicit or explicit, but they are always in play.

Consider, for instance, the teaching communities in which you participate: your department, grade-level team, Professional Learning Community, action research team, university class, or your conversations with another teacher with whom you share the joys and torments of your work. Each of these is defined by its own protocols and procedures, habits and rituals, and language practices. And they all are based on standards, values, and expectations.

This is important for us and our students to understand because while "community" is an important concept, it harbors some dangers. *Community* is one of those warm, fuzzy words that we sometimes throw around without inspecting what it really means, or what it would take to achieve it in reality. These days, for instance, we hear a lot about Professional Learning Communities (PLCs). As a concept, PLCs have a lot going for them: they suggest that teachers are reflective professionals, that they should always be learning, and that they should do so in collaboration with others—all concepts we have no trouble endorsing. But PLCs are more than a concept; they're also a *model* of staff development. We have seen PLCs thrust upon unsuspecting and sometimes resistant teachers, as if community could be achieved by administrative fiat. What we have in these situations is less professional community than what Andy Hargreaves (1995) calls "contrived collegiality," which is administratively regulated, and often compulsory, leaving little room for genuine teacher inquiry (p. 81). Moreover, sometimes the term *community* papers over important differences within a group. If individuals or subgroups within a larger group are asked to sacrifice their uniqueness, their own points of view, and their voices, then we don't have community; we have oppressive groupthink. Finally, "community" can sometimes become an excuse for insularity. If a group of people becomes hardened against the influence of other groups or forces outside of it, it stagnates, becomes exclusive, and leads to balkanization within a school (Hargreaves).

How can we avoid these dangers of community, both for ourselves and for our students? The answer, we believe, lies in careful, critical reflection by all community members about the purposes and functions of the community. The following activity is designed to elicit this kind of thinking by asking you to articulate the kind of community that best supports your teaching.

Shaping Communities

Teaching Community Charter

What is your ideal teaching community? What kind of community support would help you do your best work—as both a teacher and a professional learner? Who would be part of this community? (And who would not?) What would be the responsibilities of the members of this community? What kinds of behaviors would you and your colleagues engage in? What would be the nature of your interactions?

Write a charter for this community—a document stipulating the conditions under which it operates and the rights and responsibilities of its members. ❖

Taking part in this activity is one way to avoid the negative versions of community because it puts individual participants' needs, desires, and expectations on the table. All the negative developments described above are the result of a group that takes its own assumptions, biases, practices, procedures, and rituals—in short, its culture—for granted. This activity keeps the community honest by opening its culture up to scrutiny by all members.

The choice of a charter is not arbitrary. A charter is an authoritative document; it sets conditions and outlines terms of operation. It allows you to have your say in an explicit and empowering way. Even if you do not share your charter with colleagues, you may find this activity personally rewarding. We do, however, advise groups of teachers—as small as two friendly colleagues or as large as whole academic departments—to draft and share charters, and perhaps to compose a community charter from the overlapping tenets among the individual ones. These collaborative documents can become the focus of regular collective review and revision.

All the dangers that attend communities in general apply as well to classroom communities. They, too, are susceptible to administrative coercion (this time by the teacher), groupthink, erasure of differences, and insularity. For this reason, we often have students write a "class constitution" (Activity 5-1), which is both a valuable writing activity in its own right and a nice way to get adolescent writers thinking about the kind of community that supports their best work as writers and learners.

Activity 5-1
English Class Constitution

Together, we will write a class constitution. To constitute something means to bring it into being. For a social group such as a classroom (or a nation), this requires us to lay out the basic laws and principles that will govern our conduct, including our rights and responsibilities as "citizens."

Please begin by working in groups of three or four. Using the U.S. Constitution as your model, each group should write:

1. a short preamble that identifies the purposes of the document (this should begin, "We the People of ____...")
2. at least five articles that spell out governing rules and responsibilities of class citizens
3. a Bill of Rights (five to ten items) outlining the fundamental rights of all classroom citizens

Once each group has drafted all three pieces, we will share and craft a class constitution out of the common elements of the groups' contributions. This constitution will govern our work together; we are setting the terms of citizenship in our English class.

Teaching Writing That Matters © 2008 by Chris W. Gallagher and Amy Lee, Scholastic Professional.

Generating a class constitution invites students to reflect on the conditions that impact learning and their role in co-creating a successful learning environment. In this way, this activity invites a sense of responsibility and an awareness of the role each participant plays in shaping the community. This is a document you can return to throughout the year, practicing real and purposeful revision with your students as you check to see whether the document is flexible enough, if it failed to include an important component, and if members are living up to it. This document can be useful in setting the terms not only of whole-class interaction, but of smaller-group work too, including peer review groups or collaborative writing projects.

Of course, in order to put charters and constitutions to the test, as it were, we and our students must be able to observe, describe, and evaluate what happens in communities. This is not easy to do, but it's helpful to think of communities as texts that might be "read."

"Reading" Communities

Classroom Observation

Choose a trusted colleague whom you feel comfortable inviting into your classroom and in whose classroom you would be welcome. (This activity may be completed by groups of three or four teachers as well.)

Each of you will visit the other's classroom and gather observational data. The data collected will be determined by the questions that each teacher would like to have answered about his or her classroom. Begin individually by asking yourselves what you would like to have a better handle on in your classroom, and how having another pair of eyes in the room might help you do that.

Generate a short list of questions (begin with two or three) to guide your colleague's observations. Be sure your questions are concrete and open up to direct observations, rather than call for a general judgment. For example, instead of asking, "Is my classroom a safe space for girls?" you might have your colleague keep track of the number of times girls and boys speak in class and the nature of those responses. Or instead of asking, "Do I mix up the activities enough?" you might ask your colleague to document the range of activities she or he observes in a given class period or over a series of class periods. The key is to guide your colleague toward observing a specific dynamic or behavior in your classroom that you have a hard time observing yourself because you're so engrossed in teaching.

Before the observation, meet and discuss the questions, making sure the observer understands what to look or listen for during the class. You might want to construct a checklist, rubric, chart, or other form that will help the observer record data quickly during the observation. Finally, discuss whether and how the observer will be intro-

duced to the students, taking whatever measures are necessary to ensure that the observer's influence on the class is minimized. (For example, the observer may need to sit in the back of the class or outside a circle; we do not recommend that the observer participate in the class activities.)

During the observation, the observer should try to be as faithful as possible to the questions asked and the requested data gathering; the questions generated by the observed teacher should guide the observations and the documentation of those observations.

After each of you has visited the other's classroom (however many times you decide is necessary for answering your questions), sit down and discuss the observations. How do the observations match the observed teacher's sense of that phenomenon? Are there any surprises for the observed teacher? What conclusions might be drawn from the observations? What ideas or strategies did the observer learn? What new practices can both of you take away from the observation and conversation? ❖

This is a basic template for collegial classroom observations; obviously, it can and should be tailored to the needs of the participating teachers. But even using this simple protocol allows us to engage in informal teacher research that can lead to important insights about what is happening in our classrooms.

Note the lack of evaluative language in this activity. We have found that collegial reflection on teaching is possible only when the activity is driven by open-ended inquiry and not by evaluative judgments. Both teachers must enter the project willing and eager to learn, not to show off or compare themselves to each other.

Though the individual teacher's questions guide the observations, the step of this activity that teachers invariably find most useful and interesting is the last one, when they sit together and talk about what they saw and heard in the classroom and discuss what to make of those observations. In these moments, they are collaboratively *reading* the classroom community. At the same time, they are *forming* a teaching community of their own. They are opening their classroom doors, engaging in collaborative professional inquiry, and forging the kind of meaningful, respectful relationships that we all want for ourselves and want to model for our students.

Just as we teachers benefit from observing and analyzing the communities in which we teach, writers must do the same in the communities in and for which they write. For example, students might take "field notes" in their classes and report back to the group about their observations. In Activity 5-2, we focus on helping students "read" communities outside the classroom.

Activity 5-2
Community Event Observation

You will observe a community event or activity, taking careful notes. The event or activity should be fairly short and (of course) observable. It might be something like a church service, a club meeting, a sporting event, a town/city council meeting, a neighborhood watch meeting, or a demonstration or rally. Because we are interested in how members of this community use language, you will both observe spoken language and collect (or vividly describe) three print or visual texts. In both cases, take notes on questions such as the following:

- Who speaks and who writes in this community? Who does not?
- What kinds of speaking and writing do you observe? What forms do speakers and writers use? (Speeches, brochures, minutes, signs, posters, PowerPoint presentations, etc.) What are some of the conventions of those forms? What do those conventions say about the speakers/writers or the audience?
- What are the purposes of this speaking and writing? Who are the audiences?
- How do speakers and writers appeal to their audiences? What shared values do they invoke? What do they assume about their audience members?
- What effects do speakers and writers appear to have on their intended audiences? Are these the intended effects?

After you complete your observation, write a report, based on your notes, that introduces the language practices of this community to your classmates. Be sure to explain what this group is and does, as well as how they use language to do that work.

Teaching Writing That Matters © 2008 by Chris W. Gallagher and Amy Lee, Scholastic Professional.

Again, we find that students require more "scaffolding" than teachers do—more guidance for their observations. Because they are examining communities *as writers*, we also want students to study language use in the community. Accordingly, we provide fairly detailed, directive protocols.

Once again, this is a simple template; it could be developed and made much more elaborate. (For example, we often ask our first-year college students to note any discord or divergent values within the communities they observe; these are often, though not always, more difficult to identify and describe than shared ideas and values.) The key is to help students study how communities are formed and forged through language. This helps them understand how language functions in specific contexts, and it also helps them consider possibilities for their own writing.

Learning how to "read" communities is a crucial skill for teachers and writers. But of course it is not enough. The promise of the Writing Studies classroom is that teaching and writing are *consequential*; they make a difference in real communities of practice. We end Part II of this book, then, with activities designed to encourage you and your students to write for change.

Writing for Change

"Help Me Teach"

Identify one thing about your school, community, or state that hinders your ability to do your best teaching: a policy, structure, practice or procedure, a group, a person, and so on.

Who is in a position to change this "thing"? An administrator? The school board? Parents? Other community members? State legislators? Your U.S. congresspeople? Write a letter directly to this person or these people explaining (1) how this "thing" affects your teaching, and (2) how an action on their part would help you teach more effectively.

(Note: You could also identify something that aids your teaching or makes it easy and write a letter of praise.) ❖

As with many of the activities in this book, this one is simple, but it could have significant consequences. Even if your letter doesn't bring about the desired response, it is the mark of an engaged professional to try to shape the conditions of her work, to advocate for the best possible environment for that work. Sometimes, even writing the letter, without sending it, can help us think about the learning environment in our classrooms and schools and what we can do to help shape them. But we have found that thoughtful, respectful letters from teachers about teaching and learning are generally well received by a wide range of people, even when those people are being asked to reconsider a long-standing practice or policy. Writing for change is an act of community involvement and leadership, a way to have your say as an expert in teaching and learning. We hope you feel empowered to claim this expertise through your own writing.

In this, we believe you will find that students will follow your lead. When young people are surrounded by adults who write in ways that matter—ways that make a difference in their communities—they are more likely to view and practice writing this way themselves. Many of the writing projects in the project toolboxes in Part III are designed to encourage students to "go public" with their writing—to take their ideas and arguments outside the walls of the classroom. When they begin

> **Writing really can, and does, change the world.**

to do this, they see that writing really can, and does, change the world.

Unsurprisingly, given our discussion in Part I about the messages our culture and educational systems send young people about writing, many students need a bit of convincing. Many simply do not believe their writing can matter. For these students, it makes sense to start small, perhaps within the school community, as in Activity 5-3.

We provide an expanded version of this activity as a research project in Chapter 8, "Project Toolbox 3." It is important, of course, that students' arguments be bolstered by thoughtful research. But this shorter activity at least gets students thinking about how their writing might make a difference in their school community. To complete this activity, they must think critically about their school—*beyond* simply complaining about it—and consider how they can make a consequential contribution to it. They also must consider purpose, audience, and context.

Activity 5-3
If I Could Change One Thing

If you could change one thing about the way our school works, what would it be? Shorter classes? Longer classes? Smaller classes? Bigger classes? More free time? Longer passing periods? Longer lunch periods? Fewer tests? More computers or other technology? More nutritious lunches? Less homework? Fewer cliques? Fewer bullies? More after-school activities? A club, team, or organization you'd like to see?

Write a short letter to someone who is in a position to do something about this thing you'd like to see changed. Explain why you believe this change would be beneficial to the school. Remember your audience: You'll need to make your case in a way that your reader will find convincing. In other words, don't write a complaint letter. Your job is to convince your reader that your proposed change would make this a better school.

Teaching Writing That Matters © 2008 by Chris W. Gallagher and Amy Lee, Scholastic Professional.

Of course, not all students' letters will bring about their desired changes (nor should they; some of their ideas will be better than others!). This is a reality that all writers must face. Our job is to help our young writers see what's really important—that they are seeking connection with others through their writing. They are writing for meaningful purposes to actual readers. They are participating in their community. They are writing for change.

And we are teaching writing that matters.

PART III

Toolboxes

P art III presents three project toolboxes, one writer's process toolbox, and a
teacher's toolbox to help you and your students build your own Writing Studies
classrooms.

Why toolboxes?

Throughout this book, we have insisted on the *constructive* nature of teaching and
writing: both activities require their practitioners to design and build. We may be
handed blueprints—teach to this objective, use that graphic organizer—but if the writing and the teaching are to *matter*, we must make them our own; we must become
designers and builders.

Most builders use tools, of course. But as we have suggested, even a huge stockpile
of the best tools in the world will not help the builder who does not know what she is
building—or why. Good builders are reflective about their work: they pursue their
projects with their beliefs about building in mind. Because they are reflective practitioners, good builders weigh their options and choose the right tools for the job at
hand. They don't mindlessly follow accepted wisdom or hard-and-fast rules for building—they know each project will present new demands and challenges—but they do
learn from and contribute to the collective understandings of the community of
builders in which they work.

Many of the tools collected in Part III indeed emerged from particular teaching
communities—namely, the University of Nebraska–Lincoln Composition Program and
the University of Minnesota General College. Most
of the tools could not be traced to an individual;
instead, they are the products of the collective
efforts of many teachers working together. We are
immensely grateful to our teaching colleagues, not
only for the work they put into these tools, but also
for the ways in which their ideas and approaches to
teaching have shaped our own and are reflected
throughout this book.

This last acknowledgment is important not only
in order to recognize the extent of our indebtedness

> **Tools themselves
> do not build
> classrooms; only
> teachers and
> students, working
> together, can
> do that.**

Teaching Writing That Matters

to our colleagues, but also in order to signal the importance of teaching (in) community and the ways in which the tools themselves do not build classrooms; only teachers and students, working together, can do that. We will supply projects and tools with which we and our colleagues have experienced success, but you and your students must *put them to work* in your own classrooms.

Putting tools and projects to work begins with making choices among them—choosing the ones that best suit your purposes. But you may find yourself *retooling*, too. That is, you might use one of our tools for a job other than the one for which we fashioned it. Or you might refashion our tools, changing them for your ends. Or you might fashion tools of your own: entirely new ways to accomplish projects. We welcome retooling; it is a sign of the kind of active intelligence that characterizes teaching and writing that matter.

The three project toolboxes that follow are organized around typical kinds of work that writers do: (1) writing with experience; (2) writing with texts; and (3) writing with research. These three categories roughly correspond to typical *forms* of writing in middle school and secondary-level classrooms: personal essays (expository or narrative), critical or analytical essays, and research papers. But as you know, Writing Studies classrooms are not confined to school-based forms of writing; instead, they encourage students to engage in real-world writing in various genres for multiple purposes and audiences.

In addition, please note the preposition in each project toolbox title: *with*. That little word is important because it signals our desire, in a Writing Studies classroom, to move students out of the role of spectator of conversations, removed from their worlds, and into the role of participant in those conversations. We don't want students merely to write *about* their experiences, or texts, or research; we want them to understand these as sources of meaning, insight, and even inspiration.

> We don't want students merely to write *about* their experiences, or texts, or research; we want them to understand these as sources of meaning, insight, and even inspiration.

Think of it this way: *preposition* has the word *position* in it, and that's what preposi-tions—*above, at, below, beyond*—describe. What we're trying to describe here is the position of the writer. Writing "about" something implies that the writer is outside of that something, observing it and commenting on it. But writing "with" something positions us in a more intimate, dynamic relationship with that something: we are alongside it, in conversation with it. This, we argue, is the (dis)position that produces writing that matters.

Each project toolbox includes a brief discussion of the kind of work involved in that toolbox, a set of project descriptions, two sample projects (one designed for indi-vidual writers and the other for groups), and a set of tools: activities, strategies, and exercises you can use to help writers complete their projects.

Following the project toolboxes are a writer's process toolbox (Chapter 9) and a teacher's toolbox (Chapter 10). The writer's process toolbox includes a range of tools that support students' writing process as they undertake any kind of writing project, and the teacher's toolbox provides a variety of activities you can undertake, alone or with colleagues, as you build your Writing Studies classroom.

Chapter 6

Project Toolbox 1: Writing With Experience

Research and experience teach us that most writers do their best writing when they are somehow personally connected to the topic—when it is familiar to them and hits "close to home." As we discussed in Chapter 1, we learn *how* to write only when we *want* to write. Also, we are likely to feel more confident if we know our subject well.

For this reason, writing classes often begin by asking students to write about something personal, something with which they are intimately familiar and about which they can claim "expert" knowledge. This is also true of standardized assessments, which, as we discussed in Chapter 2, often sequence narrative and description before the supposedly more complex task of argument.

But effective experience-based writing is more complicated than we often make it out to be. In order to be effective, after all, it must go beyond simply recording or recounting events. It's not "good" simply because it's true; it's good because it does something interesting *with* experience.

The distinction between writing *with* and writing *about* experience is crucial. If we think of ourselves as writing *about* our experiences, we will approach our experience as a topic, a subject matter, a body of information that already exists, fully formed and complete with meaning that needs merely to be fished out and presented to readers. We will observe it from the outside, as spectators. As teachers, we know what kind of writing this produces. Who among us hasn't read a batch of students' personal essays or narratives and found them to be flat, unsatisfying, unfocused—without a beating heart? Who among us hasn't found ourselves bored or unconvinced by overly familiar, cliché-ridden stories like "The Big Game" or "The Time I Learned Not to Judge a Book by Its Cover"? Who among us hasn't rolled our eyes at the freeze-dried, prepackaged "morals" that these stories come wrapped in—the writing that mutters rather than matters?

The fault here lies neither in students—who are likely writing as they have been taught—or experience itself, which is always dynamic and complex. Rather, the fault lies in our approach to experience-based writing. An alternative approach to writing about experience is to write *with* it. This approach places students inside or alongside their experience, interpreting it, thinking about what it means or could mean, and then making choices about how best to render it and its significance for readers.

Writing with experience can and should stretch students as writers and knowers, helping them to develop a deeper understanding of themselves and their world. As the projects and tools offered in this toolbox illustrate, this kind of writing is really a form of re-vision: seeing again an event or events whose meaning or significance may not be entirely clear in the moment or without an occasion for extended reflection. When we think through an experience and put it into writing, we discover new insights about its meaning, about who we are (or were, or are becoming), as well as our relationships with others and the world and what has profoundly shaped us. But this potential needs to be supported and enabled through deliberate design because it won't just naturally emerge from writing about experience.

The projects that follow are intentionally designed to be flexible and suggestive, open to being inflected by and adapted for the particular context in which you teach. They are also constructed to provide writers considerable flexibility, in terms of their choice of topic and final product. But regardless of the particular design decisions you and your students make, these projects get students engaged in the intellectual and rhetorical work of writing with experience.

Projects

To facilitate the rich potential in writing with experience, the challenge for us as teachers is to compose and structure assignments that require students to wonder about, reflect on, and represent the meaning and the significance of their experience. We find it useful to ask students to think about how their writing might prompt readers to reflect, and not simply be entertained or enthralled by the experience. For example, writers might be asked to do any of the following:

- Compile a CD of eight to ten songs that have a special connection to some experience they have had or to an aspect of their identity and write liner notes, explaining what each song means to them and how it illuminates some facet of their experience or identity
- Compose an essay that explores different nicknames they have had and explains how these names communicate something important about their experience and identity
- Write a letter to someone who had a large influence on them but doesn't know it, recalling for this person a specific moment that sticks with them and explaining why
- Write three versions of the same family story, as three different people would tell it
- Write and illustrate a children's picture book about an important experience they had when they were a child

Note that most of these prompts ask students to explore more than one perspective or idea. That's by design: this is one way to encourage students not to take their experiences for granted, as though they come with preformulated meanings.

Another way is to push students to consider their intended audience, who may need to be convinced to "read" the experiences as the writer does. Thinking about audience will also help writers work through one of the central and inevitable challenges of writing with experience: deciding which details are critical and which are not, given their current purposes (which is different from asking which details were most important to the experience at the time).

Activity 6-1
Writing From Tension

This project asks you to explore a tension that has been important in your life. Think about tension like this: you produce tension in a string by pulling its ends in *opposite* directions. So a tension, for our purposes, is any idea, event, or set of forces that pulls you in different directions. For example, you could examine two competing values you hold. Or different versions of yourself that emerge or are perceived in different parts of your life (at home, on the field, at work, in class, with your friends, in the neighborhood, when you're alone). Or perhaps you have interests that show different sides of your personality, but people don't seem to expect them to coexist.

Once you've selected a tension, you'll need to dig in and do some thinking about it: When did you first realize this was a tension? Has it changed over time? What are the causes of the tension? What is its impact? Is it unique in some way to your life and experience? Or do you think this is a common tension (and if so, for whom)? Who do you think could learn from reading about your experience? What can readers learn from exploring this tension?

After you've identified your readers, a key decision will be to choose the form in which you can best reach your intended audience. For example, say you're writing about the tension you encountered in seventh grade when you wanted to hang out with new friends, but that would have meant abandoning your grade-school best friend because he just didn't fit in with your new friends. You might decide to write to your old best friend, maybe in a letter. Alternatively, you could target grade-school kids by writing a story about a kid who experiences this tension and how he makes a decision.

(Adapted from an assignment by Debbie Minter)

Teaching Writing That Matters © 2008 by Chris W. Gallagher and Amy Lee, Scholastic Professional.

By way of illustrating what these projects might look like, we offer two samples, one designed for individual writers (Activity 6-1, preceding page) and the other a collaborative project (Activity 6-2, pages 74 and 75).

Again, notice that these projects ask students to put different ideas or experiences next to each other so that they may explore multiple interpretations and meanings of experience. Students are writing from the authority that comes from their lived experience, but they are also engaging in probing inquiry into that experience. To complete the projects successfully—to move from writing *about* experience to writing *with* experience—students must move beyond what they think they know about the experience, as well as what they may have learned about experience-based writing. Some of the questions students will need to ask include:

- How can I choose an experience that is worth thinking about and writing from in the first place?
- How can I make meaning from it?
- How can I carefully select and effectively communicate details of that experience in writing? (For some students, the challenge will be including enough detail about their experience to support their interpretation; other students may struggle to select and condense the details of their experience in order to have time and space for reflection and meaning-making.)
- How can I write for a specific purpose and audience? How does my rhetorical context help me make choices about language, form, and voice so that I communicate effectively?

These can be extremely complex questions, no doubt. But they are the kinds of questions writers ask. Engaging students in this thinking, while adjusting our expectations to their specific level of experience, is critical to helping them become writers—not just students who write.

Finally, no matter what projects you assign or the age of your students, writing with experience should engage students in the kinds of work writers do when they produce effective writing with experience:

Activity 6-2
Themed Magazines

Each of you will work in a "production team" of four or five students to create a theme-based magazine for the class. This will be your general process:

1. Choose a theme for your team's magazine. The theme should relate to your experiences, and should teach readers something or reveal new aspects of the theme through the articles and features you include. Here are just a few possible themes: neighborhood, family, food, music, sports, work, and career and education decisions.

2. Once you identify your theme, you need to choose a demographic for your magazine: What age readers are you aiming to reach? Do you imagine your readers will share any kind of cultural or geographic characteristics? Are these readers new to your theme? Experienced? A range?

3. Now you need to decide on the individual articles each of your team members is going to write: What will be the specific focus of the articles? How can you be sure you have different genres (profile, review, interview, investigative article, editorial) to provide some variety throughout your publication?   ➜

- Appreciating the need to *interpret* our experiences, rather than assuming they come with prepackaged meanings
- Engaging in selection and synthesis of details
- Exploring that experience from multiple perspectives, generating multiple meanings
- Making one of those meanings significant for someone else
- Writing a text in an appropriate form to a chosen audience

You might think of these learning goals as "design specs" for students' projects. We recommend discussing learning goals with students as they embark on the work. In order to generate learning goals, ask yourself: What do I want students to know and be

4. Once you have produced the drafts of your articles, your team should conduct an editorial review: read and provide feedback on one another's drafts. Remember, while you are producing individual articles, you are also producing a single magazine to reflect the work of your team. So it's important to support one another to achieve the best product.

5. Next, you'll need to think about how you want to arrange the individual articles. What sequence or order makes the most sense or has the best effect?

6. Once you've arranged the articles, you'll need to write an editors' introduction to your magazine. This introduction should draw out the themes of the individual pieces, or explain to readers why these pieces stand as a collection, as a whole.

7. Finally, your magazine will need a cover. What design elements—colors, images, words—will communicate something to readers about what is inside? What will entice them to open it?

We will distribute the completed magazines and read them as a class.

Teaching Writing That Matters © 2008 by Chris W. Gallagher and Amy Lee, Scholastic Professional.

able to do by the end of this project? You can ask students the same question and involve them in constructing learning goals as well.

Project Tools

Of course, writers will need time and support at each step of their projects. The tools in the next section are intended to help them read their texts and craft their writing projects.

(Note: A number of the tools collected under "Invention Tools" in Chapter 9, "A Writer's Process Toolbox," are designed to help students recollect and examine their experiences.)

Naming Names

(Adapted from an activity by Debbie Minter)

1. Ask students to take out a sheet of paper and to brainstorm a list of names or labels that have been applied to them. The questions below might help them as they generate their lists.
   - What names, nicknames, and labels have family members or close friends given you? (Think through the various stages of your life.)
   - What roles do you play/have you played in your life? (troublemaker, sister, brother, teacher, clown, patient, etc.)
   - What names or labels are associated with your habits, character or personality traits, interests, or hobbies? (athlete, procrastinator, Type A, etc.)
   - What names or labels derive from memberships in groups? (Catholic, band kid, skater, etc.)
   - Any others?

2. Have students read through their list and take five to ten minutes to examine it: What is their impression of the list as a whole? What kind of person emerges from this list? Do they see patterns or surprises?

3. Once students have spent some time thinking and writing about their list, ask them to choose one name/label that has been particularly influential to their identity because it creates a tension or conflict for them. Is there a name/label that has both benefited and cost them? Is there one label they're just not sure about, uncertain whether it really fits or what it symbolizes? Have students do a bit of focused freewriting or brainstorming about how this particular name/label has affected them, for good and ill.

4. You might extend this activity by asking students to develop a short scene that dramatizes the tension in this name/label. This could be the moment of naming—when someone confers it on them or when they first come to see themselves in terms of it. Or it could be a scene in which they resist or react to it. It could also be a scene in which two people disagree about the meaning of the name/label. In any event, the scene should make clear why the name/label holds tension for the student.

Topic-Based Inventory

This tool is a particular kind of brainstorming activity. The task is simply for students to catalog their memories related to their chosen topic. So, if a student is writing about the influence of music on her life, she could push herself to recall memories of listening to music, discovering a new band, developing her musical taste and influences on her sensibility, and so on. Often, these moments lurk in the margin of our memory, having slipped beneath our conscious awareness. The idea, then, is to help students generate a richer inventory of experience from which to choose when diving into their projects. By way of illustration, this prompt asks students to brainstorm in relation to their writing lives. But we can imagine an inventory geared toward any variety of topics: music, sports, hobbies, a particular aspect of one's identity or social grouping, and so forth.

> Catalog all of the forms or genres in which you can remember ever having written. Be sure to include everyday forms such as grocery lists, e-mails, letters and thank-you notes, and recipes, as well as school writing, including research papers, personal essays, lab reports, and so on.

When students run out of ideas, they can share their lists with one another; often, students discover genres in a peer's list that should have been on their list, too. Then it will be time to analyze the lists by asking some basic questions:

- How would you describe the writer represented by this list?
- Does the list have areas of emphasis (for example, creative writing)?
- What surprises you about the list?
- What's missing from the list?
- If you were to point to one positive feature of the list, what would it be?
- If you could change one thing about the list, what would it be?

Life Stages

(Adapted from an activity by Amy Goodburn)

This activity should help students think richly about their development over time with regard to a skill, belief, attitude, value, or aspect of their identity. By way of illustration, this "stages" tool is about a student's musical life, but it could be adapted to their lives as athletes, language learners, churchgoers, siblings, and so on. The questions that follow are prompts to get students thinking; they needn't write in response to every question, but should feel free to skip around. The key is to have them do some sustained brainstorming writing, 10 to 15 minutes, on some questions in each category.

Early Childhood

- What are your earliest memories of music? What feelings are associated with these memories?
- Do you associate music from those early years with any particular people?
- Do you recall particular songs? Kinds of music?
- If you play an instrument or sing, was it your choice to do so? What do you remember about your early years of learning to do this?
- Was your learning to play or sing encouraged/valued? By whom? Why? Was it criticized? By whom? Why?
- Who listened to your earliest attempts? What do you remember about their responses?
- Where did you do most of your listening to or creating of music?

Now

- Have your musical tastes changed as you have grown older? How? Why?
- Who or what influences your musical tastes? What gets you to listen to or play new music?
- What feelings do you associate with music? Are these feelings the same or different from the ones you associated with it when you were young?
- Is your music (listening or playing) encouraged/valued? By whom? Why?
- Have your feelings about music changed? How? Why?
- Who listens to your music now? How do they respond?
- Where do you listen to music? Where do you sing/play music?
- Has the role of music-—its importance or its function—in your life changed since you were little?

Focused Freewrite: What Happened; What Does it Mean?

Part 1: What Happened

Begin by asking students to do some exploratory writing about an experience they have had in relation to their project topic. If you've asked students to begin with any of the three preceding tools, they might start this activity with those brainstorms in front of them, choosing a particular item or response as a starting point. The task of Part 1 is to isolate an important, relevant experience—one that sticks out in their memory—and to capture in writing *what happened*. Ask students to try to remember as many details as they can about this experience. Perhaps ask them to sketch out a scene: Where did this happen? Who else was there? If there had been a video camera in the room, what would it have recorded? If the project focus is students' writing lives, for example, then they might begin by freewriting about writing they've done in school or outside of school, public writing or personal writing. It could be a positive experience (connecting to a pen pal halfway across the world) or it could be a negative one (having their writing held up for ridicule by a teacher).

It isn't unusual for students to need to freewrite about several experiences before landing on one that is significant enough and that they can remember in enough detail to write about for this project.

Part 2: What Does it Mean?

Now ask students to take their brainstorming and begin to focus on exploring what this experience means to them. Why is it significant? Why has it stuck in their memory? What were the results or what was the impact of this experience? What does it tell us about them? Do they think this experience is typical? Or is there something unique about it? Encourage students to try out different interpretations of this experience, to look at it from other angles. What other explanations might there be? What might the experience have meant to the other people involved?

For example, if the project focus is students' writing lives, say a student has selected the time his fifth-grade teacher used his story as a negative example in front of the whole class. Maybe the meaning he takes from this experience is that he's never been a good writer. But what else might have been going on here? Was the teacher pointing out a common mistake, and his story just happened to be the one she used to illustrate the point? Was he already a student who struggled with writing, sure he was a bad writer and this simply confirmed it? Was the mistake not such a big deal after all? Was his teacher perhaps *wrong*? Or maybe the bigger issue is really the effect of this teaching practice on the student's attitude toward writing: Did this ridicule push him to prove something? Did it deepen his sense of failure as a writer? Did it help anyone else? What might this teacher have been thinking? What were the other students thinking?

The point is to help students explore multiple possible ways of looking at the experience, and the layers of significance and meaning that experience holds.

One-Inch Picture Frame

(Adapted from Anne Lamott's Bird by Bird *[1994] and an activity designed by Rochelle Harris)*
Anne Lamott explains this technique this way:

> Often when you sit down to write, what you have in mind is an autobiographical novel about your childhood, or a play about the immigrant experience, or a history of—oh, say—say women. But this is like trying to scale a glacier. It's hard to get your footing, and your fingertips get all red and frozen and torn up. . . . What I do at this point, as the panic mounts and the jungle drums begin beating and I realize that the well has run dry and that my future is behind me and I'm going to have to get a job only I'm completely unemployable, is to stop. First I try to breathe . . . and I finally notice the one-inch picture frame that I put on my desk to remind me of short assignments. It reminds me that all I have to do is to write down as much as I can see through a one-inch picture frame. (pp. 16–17)

This last idea is the purpose behind this writing activity: for students to move away from trying to encapsulate or capture an entire memory or experience or event, and to concentrate on a piece of it, on the fullness of a single "inch" or aspect of the whole, in order to generate depth of detail and to probe the meaning of it. Students can use this technique multiple times in relation to a single "moment" or experience, generating

Teaching Writing That Matters

many frames or pieces which can then be used as drafts or starting points for their essay. These pieces allow writers to experiment with focus, language, form, and voice as they examine an experience and its impact.

Here are the instructions we might provide to students (a slightly different, more general version appears in Chapter 9, "A Writer's Process Toolbox"):

1. Find an experience that you think you would like to write about. Spend a few moments picturing the experience from start to finish.

2. Now, pretend you have a one-inch frame that you move around to focus on a specific detail of that experience. Maybe you move it to cover a single conversation, or a single photo, or a simple moment within the larger experience. Find the small moment inside the entire experience that seems significant or meaningful to you in some way.

3. Write about just that moment. Forget about all the things you're not writing about and just focus on the one or two things in the picture frame. Think and write only about what is in the frame. Generate around 300 words (a little over a typed page). Try writing until you've covered everything in the frame.

4. If this strategy works for you, the next thing to do is move the frame to another piece of the experience and write about what shows up there. Keep doing this until you have enough material to shape your draft.

Chapter 7

❖

Project Toolbox 2: Writing With Texts

As we discuss in Chapter 1, many of our students are pretty much continuously engaged in reading and writing—though much of this work is of the fast, even *instant*, variety. Everywhere they look, it seems, they encounter texts, many of them designed by slick marketers. Follow an adolescent through a typical day and notice the number and range of texts she encounters: cereal boxes, newspapers, bumper stickers, billboards and signs, school books, school assignments, schedules and planners, posters, magazines, clothing, gossip, songs, videos, lectures, movies, text messages, e-mail messages, television shows, television advertisements (30- and 60-second), blog entries, all manner of Web sites, pop-up ads—and this is just for a start. You're also likely to see that adolescent creating a number of different kinds of texts: lists, notes, doodles, school projects, text messages, e-mail messages (instant and otherwise), blog entries, and so on.

Their constant engagement in this world of language-image-sound makes our students the most literate (some might say hyperliterate) generation ever to inhabit this planet. But again, this literacy work is mostly fast, requiring little reflection or serious deliberation. Indeed, many of the texts they—and we—encounter on a daily basis are all but invisible to us *as texts*, either because they are so ubiquitous (bumper stickers, for instance) or because we are not accustomed to thinking of them as proffering messages (clothing, say). But if we take a broad view of "text" as any unit of language, image, or sound—or a combination of these—that is intended or construed to have meaning, we begin to appreciate that our daily lives are text-soaked.

In a text-soaked world, analysis is not only an academic exercise; it is a survival skill. So, too, is the ability to write back to the texts that pervade our lives. Because our students are growing up in a world in constant conversation with itself, analyzing and participating in text-making must go hand-in-hand. It is our job to help them listen to and understand that conversation—and to join it.

Too often in school, students are asked to write only *about* texts; even when they are required to perform complex critical and literary analyses of rich pieces of literature, they remain in the spectator role. (And many students receive far thinner gruel than this, performing mechanical comprehension exercises in which they endlessly identify main ideas and supporting details of boring, scrubbed-clean "passages.") This kind of work, however cognitively complex, reinforces in students the notion that they are somehow outside the world of discourse, positioned to comment on it, but not to participate in it.

So on the one hand, students are constantly engaged in reading and writing tasks that are immediate but superficial and unreflective, and on the other, they are engaged in reading and writing tasks that are reflective and deliberative but spectatorial and "academic" in the worst sense. For most students, these two worlds are wholly separate, which is why we rarely see even the best of them transfer the analytical skills we teach in our classrooms to quotidian texts—or their academic writing skills to their non-school writing.

The solution to this problem is to ask students to write *with*, not just *about*, a wide variety of texts: everyday, academic, and literary. Writing *with* texts means writing in conversation—seeing oneself as an audience for the texts we read (which students rarely do in any authentic way in school) and then writing back, reconstituting those for whom we have been an audience into *our* audience. It brings together the reflective, deliberate work we ask students to devote to their academic analyses with the exigency and authentic purposes of their everyday work with texts.

Are adolescents ready for this complex literacy work? Are we overestimating their abilities? Isn't it enough that they *comprehend* grade-level texts? The assumption behind these questions is that students must first build their comprehension skills on simple texts (often constructed expressly to provide students with something they can read) and only then will they be prepared to do more complex work (analysis, writing back) on "real" texts (i.e., texts with actual purposes and audiences in authentic genres). But if we devote a moment's thought to our own reading experiences, we know that we understand texts better when we view ourselves as being in conversation with them, when the text speaks to us and calls forth a response from us. Many of us have had the experience of finding a book's argument completely inscrutable on a first read, but then finding it perfectly comprehensible later, when we return to it with more knowledge about the topic or an angle that helps us understand what the author is doing, or simply the motivation to understand the book (maybe because someone we respect liked it or because the information in it, we now see, is useful to us in some way). As we have insisted throughout this book, context matters.

The projects that follow are designed to help students build a shared context with the texts they read and to put themselves in conversation with those texts. This, after all, is what writers do, whether they are literary critics, essayists, book and movie reviewers, policy analysts, journalists, opinion writers, poets, screenwriters, or any number of others who write with texts. The projects and tools are adaptable across grade levels and they may be scaled up or scaled down, depending on your classroom needs and available time. In any case, the key goal of these projects is to help students experience the joys of reading, making meaning from texts, and sharing what they learn and what they think about what they learn with interested others.

Projects

Because young writers often view the world of published texts as outside their ken, it is important to design projects that offer them roles beyond that of spectator or passive responder. We favor assignments that attempt to jolt students out of that spectator role and into active conversation by expanding their notions of what texts are and what we do with them. These prompts generally provide some guidance but also considerable flexibility. For instance, young writers might be asked to do any of the following:

- Write a letter to a published author about a book that spoke to him or her in some way

- Write a play or a dialogue that puts two authors, or two characters, or an author and a character in conversation with one another
- Write a music or book review for the school or town newspaper
- Collect a "Best of . . ." set of short stories or essays (published or written by peers) and write a critical introduction explaining their choices
- Design a brochure with annotated book recommendations for summer reading or for book clubs or a citywide book reading
- Re-vision stories or essays from a different point of view, in a different setting, with a different ending, with different characters, or some other change
- Write a satire of a class reading or a popular text (a television show, for instance)
- Write a stage or film adaptation of a prose story (or the reverse)

While many of these projects might be considered "alternative"—in the sense that they are playful and ask students to view texts from unfamiliar angles—they all require the same kind of thoughtful analysis that is required by more traditional forms such as the critical or analytical academic essay. Importantly, they each offer students active roles as both readers and writers and put them into conversation with others who care about texts. In some cases, the audience is easy to discern: a brochure with summer book recommendations may be prepared for teachers, a certain grade level of students, or town libraries, for instance. In others, you may need to help students find or create forums to share their work: satires or re-visions may be collected and published, for instance, or plays may be performed for other groups of students. Students might be encouraged to submit their writing to the numerous national and regional magazines or literacy festivals that feature children's and young adults' written work.

By way of illustrating what these projects might look like, we offer two samples, one designed for individual writers (Activity 7-1)* and the other a collaborative project (Activity 7-2).

---

* Note to teachers: Though the literary form of the familiar essay took shape in the early nineteenth century among British writers such as Charles Lamb and William Hazlett, they are currently making something of a comeback. See, in particular, Fadiman (2007). Familiar essays may be found in collections such as Fadiman's *At Large and at Small* and Joseph Epstein's *With My Trousers Rolled* (1995), in general-circulation magazines such as *Harper's* and *Atlantic Monthly,* and among the "This I Believe" audio essays featured on National Public Radio and discussed in Chapter 3 of this book.

You Are What You Wear (Familiar Essays)

For this project, you will write a "familiar essay" about something, well, familiar: clothing. A familiar essay is a short, very intimate, and conversational form of writing. It begins with a person's everyday experience, but it discusses that experience in a way that explicitly connects to readers' shared concerns (not all personal essays do this). Writers of familiar essays don't necessarily know their readers personally, but they write as if they do—familiar essays are written as if they were part of a conversation among friends.

In this case, the topic of the conversation is clothing. Specifically, your job is to "read" a particular item of clothing or type of clothing for what it "says" about you:

- What does your old concert T-shirt or favorite pair of jeans or required school uniform or lucky socks or trusty pair of jeans say about who you are?
- Do you have a "look"? Does that look place you in any particular group(s)? Does it set you apart from any group(s)?
- What message does your item or type of clothing send to others? Is it associated with particular assumptions, ideas, values, or stereotypes? A certain status?

Be sure to provide ample detail about your clothing choice—you are reading it the same way we read written texts in class: for what is says and what it means. Because this is a familiar essay, your job is to talk about what the clothing means not only to you, but also to your readers, whom you don't know personally, but whom you can assume have an interest in what everyday items like clothing have to teach us about who we are.

(Adapted from an assignment by Shari Stenberg)

Teaching Writing That Matters © 2008 by Chris W. Gallagher and Amy Lee, Scholastic Professional.

Summer Reading Catalog

Working together, we will design, write, and produce a Summer Reading Catalog that we will send to our school and public libraries. The catalog will target teenage readers and will include several themes (fantasy, mysteries, beach reading, classics, etc.), depending on the books we choose to feature.

Each of you is responsible for writing three book profiles, at least one of which will make it into the final catalog. The profiles should include the following:

- a summary of the book (but avoid spoilers!) (*one paragraph*)
- a description of the target audience (*one paragraph*)
- a "One Reader's Take," which explains (again, without giving away vital information) what you liked about the book and why you think others might like it too (*two or three paragraphs*)

Our first step will be to brainstorm books to include in our catalog. This will help us avoid overlaps and begin to identify our themes. As we work on our individual profiles, we will talk about our books, share drafts of our profiles, and give each other advice. When the profiles are complete, we will vote on our final selections, ensuring that each of us has at least one profile included in the final catalog. We will also decide on design elements for the catalog: a cover, the order of the profiles, any graphics or images we might like to use (reproductions of the book covers, for instance), and the like. If we decide to make a fancy catalog, we may need to appoint or elect a production team to take the lead on this part of the work.

We will set clear deadlines for each step of the process so that by the end of the semester, we can deliver our catalogs to the librarians and celebrate our good work!

Students generally find these kinds of projects fun. But make no mistake: writing-with-texts projects present considerable challenges to adolescent writers. For a start, consider the reading practices called for by projects like these. To complete these projects successfully, students must read texts for each of these elements:

- *What they say:* the literal level
- *What they mean:* the inferential level
- *How they work:* the rhetorical level

That third level, of course, is the challenge of the Writing Studies classroom: students are asked to understand not only what texts say and what they mean, but also how they are put together (how they work internally) and their stakes and consequences in the world (how they work externally).

And that's all on the reading side. Then we ask students to formulate their own ideas, judgments, and arguments about the texts and to share those with others. Your assignment may answer some of the following questions for students, but in any case, as writers, they will need to contend with all of them:

- How can I choose a text that is worth thinking and writing about in the first place?
- What does this text say? What does it mean? How does it work?
- What do I think about the text? What ideas, judgments, and arguments can I arrive at in conversation with this text?
- With whom can I share my ideas, judgments, and arguments about this text?
- In what form can I share these ideas, judgments, and arguments?
- What strategies should I use to reach my audience?

These questions can be daunting for younger students, but they are writers' questions, and they help students develop writers' habits of mind.

Finally, then, no matter the specific assignment and no matter the age or abilities of your students, writing with texts should engage them in the kinds of intellectual work that writers do:

- Reading with understanding (literal, inferential, rhetorical)
- Rendering complex judgments about what they read

- Putting their own ideas in conversation with those offered in texts
- Shaping ideas, judgments, and arguments in conversation with texts for real purposes and audiences

You might think of these learning goals as "design specs" for students' projects. We recommend discussing learning goals with students as they embark on the work. In order to generate learning goals, ask yourself: What do I want students to know and be able to do by the end of this project? You can ask students the same question and involve them in constructing learning goals as well.

Project Tools

Of course, writers will need time and support at each step of their projects. The tools in the next section are intended to help them read their texts and craft their writing projects.

Rhetorical Analysis

This activity may be used with any kind of text that students encounter, from everyday public texts to complex academic ones. The questions below could guide classroom discussion.

- *Purpose:* What work is this text intended to do? Why was it written? What are the writer's goals? How can you tell?
- *Audience:* Who is this text intended to reach? Does it have multiple audiences, or just one? Does it have a primary (immediate) audience and a secondary (indirect or distant) audience? How does the writer show audience awareness? Is the audience addressed directly in the piece, or is it only hinted at? Does the writer implicitly or explicitly invoke the beliefs, values, assumptions, or arguments of the audience?
- *Situation:* What factors outside the text shape it? How about when and where it was written? Or when and where it was/is read? The means of circulating the text? The medium? The available technology? The existing conversation about the writer's topic?

- *Form:* What genre is this text? Why did the writer choose this genre? What are the conventions of this genre? Does the writer break any of these conventions? If so, why and with what effect?
- *Language:* Is the language of the text simple or complex? General or specialized? Why? Is this appropriate to the writer's purpose, audience, and situation?

Bumper Stickers

This activity is designed to help students analyze a particular kind of everyday text: bumper stickers. Begin by bringing a range of bumper stickers into class (physical stickers themselves or images from the Internet), or asking students to watch for them for a couple of days and then to describe or draw the ones they can remember. You could also have them design their own bumper stickers. In any case, this tool works best when you have a wide range of stickers available, from the patriotic, flag-themed ones such as "So much to be thankful for" or "These colors don't run" to declarations such as "I think, therefore I'm dangerous" or "If you're not outraged, you're not paying attention" to (supposedly) humorous ones such as "My kid can beat up your honor student" or "Homer Simpson '08."

Ask students to survey the range of bumper stickers. Here are a number of short writing exercises you might ask them to complete:

- Write a note to a friend who would love one of the stickers. Tell this friend why the bumper sticker made you think of him or her, and why you think he or she would love it.
- Write a note to a friend who would hate one of the bumper stickers. Tell this friend why the bumper sticker made you think of him or her, and why you think he or she would hate it.
- Write a character sketch for the owner of a car displaying one of these bumper stickers. What kind of car does this person drive? What does he or she do for a living? What kind of personality does he or she have?
- Two cars, each one displaying one of the bumper stickers, are involved in a minor traffic accident. While inspecting the damage, each driver notices the other's sticker. What do they say to each other?

- Name a make and model of car on which you might expect to see each sticker displayed and explain your choices.
- Design your own bumper sticker that responds to one of the others. (For example, the "My kid can beat up your honor student" sticker is a response to the popular "My kid is an honor student" sticker.)

Each of these activities asks students to interpret and analyze everyday texts, and also to share their ideas about those texts with others. The activities can often lead to engaging and productive classroom conversations about how a particular genre works, how words and images together can contribute to the meaning of a text, and how these short, pithy texts tell us something (sometimes something misleading) about the identity of those who place them on their vehicles.

Activity 7-3
Hot-Spotting

1. As you read the text, highlight, underline, place a star beside, or copy onto a fresh sheet of paper passages that really "work" for you. This could include a thought-provoking paragraph or sentence, a funny scene, a strong or compelling image, or even a word that strikes you as well used.

2. When you have completed the reading, examine the hot spots and ask yourself:
   - Why does each passage work? What makes it effective?
   - What do the passages have in common? Are there any trends in these hot spots?
   - What can I learn from these hot spots as a writer? How can I create this kind of energy in my own text?

3. Now write. Don't try to imitate the hot spots you've examined, but keep them in mind and try to write with the kind of energy you found in those compelling passages. See if you can create for your readers the same kind of experiences that the writer gave you.

Teaching Writing That Matters © 2008 by Chris W. Gallagher and Amy Lee, Scholastic Professional.

Hot-Spotting

The purpose of the hot-spotting tool (Activity 7-3, page 92) is to identify and investigate particularly effective passages in texts. This exercise often leads young writers to important insights and strategies for making their own texts more effective. In Chapter 9, "A Writer's Process Toolbox," you will find a version of this tool designed for students who are working on their own projects (Activity 9-12); there hot-spotting is a revision tool that is also helpful in promoting peer feedback.

Trouble-Spotting

Like hot-spotting, this tool (Activity 7-4) begins with the identification of particular passages in a text—only this time, the "spot" is not hot; it's cold. Or, at least, it gives

---

Activity 7-4
Trouble-Spotting

1. As you read the text, highlight, underline, place a question mark beside, or copy onto a fresh sheet of paper passages that don't "work" for you. These might include a confusing argument or leap of logic, an awkward metaphor, a grammatically-challenged sentence, a joke that falls flat, or even a word that seems out of place or misused.

2. When you've completed the reading, examine the trouble spots and ask yourself:
   - Why doesn't each passage work? Why does it give me trouble?
   - What do the passages have in common? Are there any trends in these trouble spots?
   - What might the writer be going for here? What would I need to know, or what kind of reader would I need to be, to better understand this passage?
   - What can I learn from these trouble spots as a writer? How can I avoid trouble spots in my own writing?

3. Now write, keeping these potential trouble spots in mind.

Teaching Writing That Matters © 2008 by Chris W. Gallagher and Amy Lee, Scholastic Professional.

---

the reader trouble. It confuses her or makes her wonder; it creates some sort of difficulty for her.

This tool comes with a caveat. It's tempting to consider "difficulty" to be a negative thing in reading and writing—something to be excised at all costs. Granted, no writer (outside of some avant-gardists) wishes to confuse or frustrate readers. But for writers and readers alike, difficulty is often an opportunity, a prompt toward deeper thought or a viable alternative perspective (Salvatori & Donahue, 2005; Lecourt and the UMass Writing Program Collective, 2005). Often, when we read, we skim the passages that give us trouble and focus only on those that make immediate sense to us or that resonate with us in some way. But it is often (not always) in the difficulty that the most important opportunities for learning reside. One of the virtues of this tool—if we are not too quick to write off difficulty as an unnecessary and embarrassing problem—is that it allows us to investigate difficulty and its causes.

Glossing

This tool (Activity 7-5) aids students' comprehension and helps them "talk back to" or put themselves in conversation with a text. Additionally, it focuses their attention on both what a text says and what it does. Glossing may be used on any kind of text, but is especially helpful with shorter pieces. You may also consider having students gloss their own drafts; used as a revision tool, glossing often helps students gain distance from their texts and view them in new ways.

This tool could be simplified so that students are asked to perform one or the other kind of gloss described here. In any case, it is often helpful to have students share and discuss their glosses on the same text with partners or in small groups. Comparing glosses can help make visible to students their own reading and interpreting practices.

Believing and Doubting Games

This tool (Activity 7-6) is a reading activity that is intended to help students read carefully and fully and to avoid simply scanning sources for useful information or for material with which to agree or disagree. It is based on Peter Elbow's thinking in his book *Writing Without Teachers* (1973). A key to this activity is to have students read the text *twice*.

Teaching Writing That Matters

Glossing

1. If you can write on the text you are reading, you will be using both the left and the right margins. If you cannot, you will be using a separate piece of paper, on which you should draw a line down the middle.

2. As you read the text, you will provide two kinds of "glosses," or short summary statements or phrases. On the left side of the page, you will gloss what each chunk of text (a paragraph for a shorter piece, a section for a longer one) says; basically, you will summarize the content. On the right side, you will gloss what that chunk of text does; in other words, what it adds to what you already know, or how it builds on what came before it or sets up what might come after it. Here is an example.

What It Says	**Text**	**What It Does**
Joel not much older than the narrator, but seems like it; narrator admires him.	Joel was two years older than I was, but those two years seemed to make all the difference: he was taller, stronger, smarter, more *worldly*. He had been places, done things. Far-away places, important things. I'd never have admitted it, but I looked up to him, wanted to be like him.	*Introduces Joel, but also narrator—and the relationship.*
Something bad happens, changing narrator's view.	Until that day. I learned a lot that day—about Joel, about me, about friendship, and most of all about things you can never take back.	*Creates suspense; makes us wonder what happened.*
Narrator learned important life lessons, but wasn't ready to.	Maybe what I learned that day made me smarter and more worldly. But I was still a kid, and it was too soon.	*Gives us what he learned before telling us what happened—again in suspenseful language.*
		Creates sympathy for narrator (victim of something), distrust in Joel.

3. Once you complete your glosses, you will have a kind of "map" of the text. You can examine how the story or argument develops in two ways: first ➔

on the level of content, and second on the level of structure or organization. Read over the glosses, and ask yourself:

- How does this story or idea develop? Does it make sense? Is it easy to follow? Are there any gaps? Any places where the writing seems to wander? How about places where the text seems to repeat itself?

- How is the story or idea put together? How does each chunk contribute to the overall text? Are you ever surprised or confused by what a chunk of text does?

- What if this text were arranged differently? What if it started or ended at a different place? What if some of the paragraphs or sections were omitted? How would each change affect your reading of this text?

(Adapted from Kenneth Bruffee's descriptive outlines in A Short Course in Writing, *1993)*

Activity 7-6

Believing/Doubting Game

Read the text twice:

1. The first time through, do your best to read the text on its own terms—that is, to believe it, trust it. Assume what the author assumes, think what he or she thinks. Try to figure out why the author believes what he or she believes. Write a short summary as if you were the author.

2. The second time through, read the text skeptically, doubting its assumptions and arguments. Challenge the writer, stubbornly refusing to take anything for granted. Write a short response to the text as if you were a hostile reader.

(Adapted from Peter Elbow, Writing Without Teachers, *1973)*

Teaching Writing That Matters

This tool not only encourages deliberate, thorough reading practices but also helps students understand that how they read—and how they experience a text and its arguments—is determined by their perspective. This is a critical notion for young readers, who are accustomed to reading quickly for information.

Students tend to enjoy playing this "game" and taking on different roles as readers. Some teachers ask students to work together to construct their two readings. In any case, after completing this activity, you might consider engaging your students in a classroom conversation about how different reading strategies help us arrive at different readings.

Chapter 8

Project Toolbox 3:
Writing With Research

Humans are driven by a need to know. We naturally crave information and ideas. We desire to understand the world around us.

Okay, so maybe not all of our students are poster children for these facts of life. But listen to even the most academically disengaged among them talk about the music they love, the movies they've seen, the sports they participate in or watch. Consider how much they know about these things and the passion they have for knowing and sharing that knowledge. How did that student learn so much about the different subgenres of hip-hop music? How did that one come to know so much about kung-fu films? How did this one memorize all those football stats?

But keep listening: it's not just that they know a lot (certainly more than many adults give them credit for); they also know how to use what they know to participate in conversations—including making impassioned arguments. That student is making the case that alternative hip-hop shouldn't even be compared to gangsta rap because they're so different. That one claims you can "totally tell" the lead in the movie he saw last weekend was an actor trying to do martial arts, not a martial artist trying to act (and everyone knows the latter is preferable!). This one's saying that, all right, maybe Randy Moss had a great year with his record-setting 23 NFL touchdown catches, but Jerry Rice caught his 22 in 14 games, not 16!

Seemingly idle conversations such as these are easy to dismiss, revolving as they do around preferences, including consumer choices, whose stakes do not seem terribly high. But these conversations feature all of the intellectual architecture, if you will, of the conversations that play out in sober news shows, sophisticated opinion magazines, and even austere scholarly journals. Like the participants in these forums, our students are gathering information and ideas (usually from multiple sources), analyzing and synthesizing that material, formulating their own judgments about the topics at hand, and sharing those informed judgments with others. (For more on the connections between students' informal arguments and our expectations for academic ones, see Graff, 2003.)

As we have argued throughout this book, students are routinely, and often without knowing it, engaged in incipient forms of just the sort of intellectual work we hope to encourage them to do in our classes. True, they often do this work without much depth and regarding topics we are unlikely to find suitably "academic." But when we push students to develop their research skills—asking them to dig deeper into supposedly weightier subjects—we often make the work "academic" in a negative sense. That is, we teach skills and topics in a way that removes them from students' own interests and passions. Too often in school, we present research as a set of discrete, often mechanical and lifeless skills (record bibliographic information, fill out index cards, write an outline, use proper quotation conventions, learn citation methods, and so on). Those skills are important, of course, but only in the service of meaningful intellectual work.

In other words, we often teach as though the purpose of "doing" research is to learn research skills, when the truth is something like the opposite: we learn research skills in order to conduct meaningful, consequential research—and to share with others what we learn. For example, the purpose of drawing on multiple sources of information is not to show that we can draw on multiple sources of information; it's to arrive at a more informed position and to communicate it to others more compellingly.

Of course, different rhetorical situations call for different amounts and kinds of research. An informal cafeteria conversation about football will have different requirements than a more rigorous, formal examination of the same topic on an ESPN show, and a cultural studies scholarly journal will have different requirements than either of those. Once again, context matters. Our purposes, audiences, and genres (forms) determine the kinds of research we will need to do and how we will need to use that research as we enter the conversation. Like writing itself, research is not a generic, all-purpose set of user skills; it is a social practice that writers undertake in reflective, rhetorically aware, and community-minded ways.

This explains why we prefer the phrase "writing *with* research" to the more conventional formulations of "research writing" or "writing *about* research." "Research writing" implies that we are dealing with a distinct *type* of writing—such as the "research paper" (a strictly school-based form). "Writing about research" suggests that the research we do is the *topic* of our writing, when in fact it is the question-formulating, thinking, and information-gathering that we do in service of exploring our topic. On the other hand, "writing *with* research" connotes that we use our research to further our writing goals. In addition, this formulation suggests that we are participating in conversation with others, rather than taking a spectator's or commentator's role.

The projects in this toolbox are designed to motivate students to tap into their natural desire to know, to build upon their existing research skills, and to develop writing projects that *matter*. They are intended to get (or keep) students excited about research and to share what they learn through that research. Completing projects such as these will help students develop the skills we hope to inculcate through traditional "research papers," but because the final products are in genuine forms for real audiences, rather than in this strictly school-based genre, they are far more likely to motivate students' interest and propel them to improve their writing performance.

These projects and the tools that follow them are adaptable across grade levels, and they may be scaled up or scaled down, depending on your classroom needs and available time. The key goal of these projects is to help students experience the joys of conducting research, making meaning from it, and sharing what they learn, and what they think about what they learn, with interested others.

Projects

Because writers write (and learn) best when they are personally invested in their topics, we advise crafting assignments that encourage students to formulate and investigate questions they care about. We prefer project prompts that provide some guidance but also considerable flexibility. For example, young writers might be asked to research events and issues such as these:

- The influence of an historical event—such as a war, an epidemic, a natural disaster, a law or public policy, or an invention—on their family[*]
- An issue or problem currently affecting their school
- The historical and contemporary significance of a particular building or event in their town/city
- The issues and perspectives behind a controversy currently unfolding in their hometown
- The history and purpose of an organization or group in their community
- The meaning and lineage of their name
- The life story of an elderly relative or acquaintance

Notice that the writer has a personal stake in these topics; either directly or indirectly, these topics impact the writer. At the same time, these topics open into larger conversations and controversies; they put the writer in conversation with others who have a stake in the topic. This connection between the personal and the public is immensely important for young writers trying to find their voice in the world beyond the classroom. The research process will come alive for writers only if it helps them pursue a genuine question that has meaning for them *and* for others.

By way of illustrating what these projects might look like, we offer two samples, one designed for individual writers (Activity 8-1) and the other a collaborative project (Activity 8-2).

Whatever your specific assignment, students will need your help on several of the key tasks. For example, framing meaningful research questions is often difficult, especially for younger writers. But we can model for them the kinds of questions that are complex enough to be worthy of sustained inquiry yet not so complex that students have no hope of gathering enough interesting, useful, and directly relevant information to form their own opinions about the topic. Activity 8-1 provides examples within the assignment itself, for instance.

---

[*] See Goodburn (2001) for a detailed description and discussion of family/community history projects.

Teaching Writing That Matters

Activity 8-1
Improving My School

Have you ever wondered why things are done the way they are in our school? Have you ever wished they were done differently? Here's your chance to explore an issue, a practice, or a problem that you see in our school.

The specific topic is up to you. The only requirements are these: (1) that you care about it, (2) that other people are also affected by it, and (3) that there is more than one way to look at it.

We will do some in-class activities to help you identify potential topics. The key will be to frame a research question that does not have a simple yes/no answer. Here are some examples:

- What are the benefits and drawbacks of a school dress code?
- Where do we draw the line in terms of appropriate material for a school newspaper?
- What is the nutritional value of school lunches? Who decides?
- How big a problem is bullying in our school? What effects does bullying have on students' experiences in school?
- How big a problem are cliques in our school? What effects do cliques have on students' experiences in school?
- Why are our classes the length that they are? How long are classes in other schools, and what are the benefits and drawbacks of these different options?
- What is one class that students at this school wish they could take but can't? Do any other schools offer that class? If so, do students there like it?
- Who gets into Advanced Placement/International Baccalaureate/Honors classes at this school? Who decides? Why is this the policy?

Don't be afraid to choose a topic that you don't know a lot about; that's why we do research! ➜

Once you have identified a substantive question, you will gather various kinds of information, including at least the following:

1. An interview with someone directly affected by your topic
2. An observation of a person or people being affected by your topic
3. A school document about your topic—for example, a school policy, Web site, brochure, newsletter, or memo
4. An outside source that sheds light on your topic—a national Web site, magazine article, book, and so on

When your research is complete, you will write three short pieces that use your research to present your own opinion on your topic to three different audiences. For example, if you had researched a proposed dress code, you might write a letter to the local school board, an editorial addressed to students for your school newspaper, and a sample policy statement for your school administrators. In class, we will brainstorm a list of possible forms and audiences for your pieces.

Similarly, we can help young writers understand that different sources provide varying kinds (and quality) of information. We suggest having students collect information from at least two distinctly different kinds of sources for each project. For example, for the first topic on the list on page 102—how an historical event influenced their family—students might be asked to use (1) commentaries on the event itself (books, articles, Web sites, and the like), (2) historical artifacts dealing with the event at the time it happened (photographs, advertisements, speeches, campaign posters or buttons, pamphlets, diaries, letters, town ordinances, and so on), and (3) interviews with members of their family. In addition to using both primary and secondary research methods, students may be directed to use a variety of media, including print and online, as well as a diversity of perspectives, including mainstream and alternative points of view.

Newsletter

Working together, our class will produce a newsletter for a group, organization, or agency that we will choose. Our newsletter will be distributed to the members of the group. We will work through each step of the process together, but the following are the basic steps we will take:

1. Brainstorm a list of potential "clients," including local nonprofit agencies, community programs, or clubs, organizations, and groups at our school. Who could use a newsletter, or who already has a newsletter but could use our help?

2. Arrange a planning meeting with representatives of the organization, group, or program. What will be the purpose of the newsletter? (Do they need volunteers, resources, awareness of pressing issues, more sense of community and celebration?) When should it be complete? How many pages should it be? Who will pay production and copying costs, if there are any? How will it be disseminated?

3. Learn some background on our client. If they have (or had) a newsletter, we will read some back issues. In any case, we will need to get to know our client: Why does the organization or group exist? What work does it do? Whose interests does it represent? How long has it been in existence?

4. In consultation with members of the agency, group, community, or program, determine what specific topics we'll cover in the newsletter and how much space will be devoted to each. At this point, we will elect a "production team," which will be in charge of layout and production of the newsletter. Does anyone in the class have special expertise in this area? Would learning such skills be of particular interest to anyone?

5. Planning meeting: We will map out all the potential pieces, including what each will require in terms of research (interviews, a site visit, library or   ➜

Internet research, a survey, etc.), special requirements such as photographs, and deadlines. (We will need to leave plenty of time for final editing and production of the newsletter.)

6. We will work in teams of two or three on the pieces. One we choose teams and assign stories, each team will write a plan for completing its piece.

7. As we work on our pieces, we will have plenty of time to report to one another on our progress and to give each other advice. We will also make at least one more visit (preferably more) to the client.

8. Touching base: After a couple weeks of group work, we will meet again as a large group, and each team will briefly summarize its piece, including the purpose and audience, the general approach, the research involved, and the style. This will allow us to envision what the whole newsletter will look like when completed and to see if we have any gaps or overlaps. We will also adjust space allotments if we need to at this point.

9. We will spend lots of time in class sharing drafts both within teams and in random groups. Each piece will be revised at least once, and probably more than that.

10. Final-layout meeting: When the drafts are near completion, we will meet once more to determine the layout of the newsletter—that is, what goes where. This will allow us to assign final word counts for each piece. The production team will present us with its ideas about special layout features such as a banner, title typography, photography, a table of contents, and the like.

11. Each team will be expected to do close and attentive editing for grammar, spelling, word count, and so on. Each team is also responsible for submitting its piece to the production team by the deadline.

12. The production team will assemble the final product and arrange final printing.

13. We will make a trip to the client to present copies of the newsletter in person and to celebrate our hard work.

Helping students develop this intellectual habit of considering a range of information and perspectives is not only an important academic exercise; it is also the foundation of more successful—that is, compelling, thorough, convincing—research projects. The goal, after all, is to produce research-based writing that *matters*—both to the writer and to an identifiable audience. Irrespective of topic, then, it is important to ask students to make their research meaningful to real readers. Their ultimate goal is to develop a stance on their topic and share what they've learned and what they think for a particular (expository or persuasive) purpose. We can guide them by asking them to consider questions such as these:

- What have I learned through this research?
- What do I know and believe about my topic now?
- What can I do with what I know and believe about my topic?
- Who needs to hear what I know and believe? Who is in a position to act on it?
- How can I best reach that audience? What forms or genres are available to me?
- What writing strategies can best help me accomplish my goals?

Writing with research matters when students who have to say something become writers who have something to say. Finally, then, writing with research should engage students in the kinds of intellectual work that writers do, including these processes:

- Framing a meaningful research topic/question
- Using appropriate (usually multiple) research methods to gather information
- Analyzing and evaluating different sources of information and points of view
- Synthesizing research and formulating their own stance on the topic
- Shaping research-based ideas and arguments for specific audiences and purposes

You might think of these learning goals as "design specs" for students' projects. We recommend discussing learning goals with students as they embark on the work. In order to generate learning goals, ask yourself: What do I want students to know and be able to do by the end of this project? You can ask students the same question and involve them in constructing learning goals as well.

Project Tools

Of course, writers will need time and support at each step of their projects. The tools in the next section are intended to help them conduct their research and craft their projects.

Double-Entry Notebook

This tool (Activity 8-3), based on Ann E. Berthoff's work in *The Making of Meaning* (1981), helps students record and reflect on information from various sources. They can use it for "field notes" if they conduct observational research or interviews, or as they read texts of all kinds.

Activity 8-3
Double-Entry Notebook

Using a two-column format, record notes (including direct quotations and page numbers when appropriate) on the left side of the notebook page, moving quickly to capture the important ideas in what we are viewing or reading. After completing the reading, interview, or observation, return to your notebook and use the right side of the page to respond to, extend, or question your notes.

Here are two examples of what a double-entry notebook might look like:

EXAMPLE 1

Notes	Reflections
Ehlenberg, Nancy. Personal Interview, June 4, 2008.	
At work when she first heard. Coworker turned on TV. Watched as second tower came down.	This is one of those events that everyone remembers where they were.
"I couldn't convince myself it was really happening."	I've heard this a lot.
Cried all day.	→

Still can't understand "why anyone would take all those innocent lives."

Me neither.

Thought of niece Cindy in NY. Knew she wasn't anywhere near the Trade Center, but "no one was thinking straight that day."

Everyone seemed to think of their family, even if they weren't directly involved. Maybe that's what we always do when something major like this happens. That's interesting—world-changing events are always family-changing.

"Every American family was changed on 9/11."

EXAMPLE 2

Notes

Reflections

Sacks, Peter. *Standardized Minds.* Cambridge, MA: Perseus Books, 1999.

Intro: explains "American fascination" (1) with testing. Testing is popular b/c it seems to support our ideas about "meritocracy."

Here's what I'm trying to figure out: why is testing so popular? Seems like this book will help.

Asks questions like "Whose interests does mental testing serve?" (2)

Never thought about this: maybe all this testing isn't about teaching & learning?

We shouldn't accept legitimacy of tests on faith.

Calls standardized tests "emotional and intellectual abuse" (2).

Bold statement. Definitely never thought of tests this way before, but know I've FELT this way when taking them.

Answer to question above: "America's elites" and test companies (2).

Says bk is for general audience, including parents, students, policymakers (3).

➜

Notice that double-entry notebooks require many conventional skills, including recording full bibliographic information, summarizing, paraphrasing, quoting, and so on. Students will need assistance developing these skills as they undertake this work. Here are a couple of helpful online resources:

- http://www.ode.state.or.us/teachlearn/real/documents/CMParaphrasing,-Summarizing-&-Quoting.doc
- http://books.heinemann.com/shared/onlineresources/E00797/chapter2.pdf

Annotating

Some teachers require their students to hand in annotations with their research projects because annotations are useful tools in the process of analyzing and keeping track of research. If your class is reading a book or an article together, you could ask students to write annotations of it, or of a particular chapter or section (see Activity 8-4). It is often instructive to consider how different the annotations can be, even when students are "merely" summarizing.

Interviewing

Interviewing is more difficult and complex than many students expect. They will need to practice formulating clear and useful questions and conducting interviews. Many teachers ask students to interview each other as a dry run before doing "live" interviews with people outside the classroom.

Activity 8-4
Annotating

Annotations are a kind of note taking. They are short (paragraph-long) "blurbs" that capture the essence of a source. A good annotation does three things:

1. Gives full bibliographic information
2. Summarizes the source carefully and accurately
3. Evaluates whether and how the source is useful for the research project

Here are two sample annotations:

Macy, Sue. *Swifter, Higher, Stronger: A Photographic History of the Summer Olympics*. Washington, D.C.: National Geographic, 2004.

> This is a very informative book with an awesome photo gallery. I came across it when I was researching drugs in sports, but honestly I picked it up to look at the pictures. As I expected, it has interesting chapters with titles like "Breakthrough Athletes" and "Unlikely Heroes." These talk about important people in the history of the Olympics, some famous and some not. But there's also a chapter about scandals called "Controversies Cast a Shadow." This chapter specifically talks about drugs in the Olympics, and so it will be useful to me. I can include something about the Olympics' "anti-doping" program and use a few examples from the history of the Olympic games, which now that I think about it, is really important because it's the "world's games" and everyone knows about it.

Sacks, Peter. *Standardized Minds*. Cambridge, MA: Perseus Books, 1999.

> Written by a journalist for a general audience, this book explains and criticizes this country's "fascination" with standardized testing. The main argument is that standardized testing is good for elites in this country and for the testing industry especially, but not for teachers or kids. He also argues that testing supports the idea of "meritocracy," allowing us to sort people. Sacks critiques the whole idea of test-driven accountability in schools, and offers examples ➜

of alternative approaches, including "performance assessments" that ask students to DO something meaningful rather than fill in bubbles on test sheets. Sacks's overall argument, especially Ch. 4 on "the test-driven accountability machine" (65) is important to my research because I'm trying to figure out why we have all this testing. But if I end up proposing specific solutions, his ideas about performance assessments and saying "no" to standardized tests in Ch. 11 could be useful, too.

One way to organize such an activity is to have students interview each other about a simple topic, such as their favorite hobbies. You might ask them to formulate five questions to try out with a partner. In addition to helping students become more comfortable with interviewing, this activity also provides an opportunity to examine the clarity and usefulness of their questions.

It is helpful then to ask students to interview two or more classmates on a somewhat more complex or controversial topic. To extend the example in Activity 8-1, you could ask them to craft five questions that they will pose to two classmates about their views on a school dress code. It is likely that students will find this task more difficult. You might first have them consider the merits and demerits of questions like these:

- Do you or do you not think dress codes are a good or bad idea?
- Don't you agree that dress codes are against freedom of expression?
- Are dress codes a way of making students behave better or will they make them behave worse because they will be mad at the policy?

Collective examination of questions such as these will reveal some of the common problems interviewers often encounter or create (confusing, leading, or overly restrictive questions, for instance).

It's important to help students learn to craft questions that are likely to elicit the kinds of information they really want. For instance, we can discuss with students the difference between open-ended and closed questions. They could discuss the benefits and limitations of questions such as these, for instance:

- Were you scared when you heard you were going to Iraq?
- What went through your mind when you learned about your deployment to Iraq?

Students will need help preparing for the interview itself, as well. Activity 8-5 offers a handful of tips you might suggest to them.

Activity 8-5

Tips for Interviewing

- Arrange the interview at a convenient time and a comfortable place for both you and your interviewee.
- Decide beforehand how you will record the interview. Will you rely on your notes? Will you audio-record the interview?
- Whichever recording device you use, ask your interviewee at the beginning of the interview if he or she is comfortable with it.
- Do your homework: know something about your interviewee.
- Practice asking your questions to various people. Make sure your questions are designed to elicit the kind of information you want.
- Create "probes": follow-up questions or prompts designed to keep the interviewee talking. (Examples: "Could you give an example?" "Tell me more about that experience." "Why do you say that?")
- During the interview, try to keep interviewees on track; if they stray too far from your topic, gently lead them back by asking the next question.
- Make sure you ask all of your questions, unless it is clear that the interviewee has already answered a question while responding to a previous one.
- At the conclusion of the interview, thank your interviewee for his or her time.

Teaching Writing That Matters © 2008 by Chris W. Gallagher and Amy Lee, Scholastic Professional.

Evaluating the Credibility of Sources

One of the most important tasks for any researcher is evaluating the credibility of sources. With so much information available at their fingertips, students need strategies for slowing down their reading and determining not only the value, but also the accuracy of what they read. A number of universities have developed helpful resources for evaluating Internet sources in particular:

- Purdue University: http://www.lib.purdue.edu/ugrl/staff/sharkey/interneteval/
- University of British Columbia: http://www.library.ubc.ca/home/evaluating/
- Georgetown University: http://library.georgetown.edu/internet/eval.htm

Though they vary somewhat, and though they raise concerns specific to Internet sources, these resources can help us think about how to guide students' evaluation of sources they use for their research projects. Here are the kinds of questions these sites urge us to ask of sources:

- Who is the author? What are the author's credentials? Position? Institutional/organizational affiliation?
- Is the information *accurate*? Is it consistent with information from other credible sources?
- Is the information *objective*? What are the sources of the information? Are those sources biased? For example, if the authors rely on studies, who conducted those studies? Are those researchers independent or paid consultants? Are they associated with a university or a think tank?
- Is the information *current*? When was the copyright granted? If the source is a Web page, when was it last updated? Does the source cover the most recent developments about your topic?
- Is the information *comprehensive*? Is it based on multiple sources of data, or only selected ones? Does it account for multiple points of view, or only one narrow one? Does it present the whole story?

Avoiding Plagiarism

When we think of plagiarism, we tend to think of outright cheating: a student downloading a paper from the Internet and handing it in as his or her own work. This certainly qualifies as plagiarism, and of the most flagrant and distressing sort. But it is important to remember that plagiarism comes in many forms, and can be either intentional or unintentional. Sometimes, to be sure, students are trying to get away with something. But often, they are unaware that they are not citing sources appropriately or fully. This is especially so for students from other cultures, where different notions of intellectual property and intellectual integrity may govern academic work.

None of this is meant to excuse plagiarism. Instead, we call attention to the complexity of plagiarism because doing so reminds us that plagiarism and avoiding plagiarism are intellectual, social, and cultural practices that require more attention than a simple list of dos and don'ts.

In the sidebar, we provide some teaching strategies that can help discourage plagiarism. Note how well these strategies fit with the approach to teaching writing that we advocate in this book; as it turns out, effective strategies for teaching writing are also effective deterrents to student plagiarism. A larger and perhaps obvious point is that when students are motivated to write, when they *care* about their writing, they are less likely to resort to plagiarism.

Teaching Strategies to Discourage Plagiarism

- Discuss the concepts of intellectual property and academic integrity with writers (some writing handbooks have chapters on these topics). Instead of simply providing writers with rules, help them understand *why* we provide information about our sources (to acknowledge the origin of ideas, to respect intellectual property, to provide readers with further resources, and so on).
- Help writers understand how to use sources in their writing: practice summary, paraphrase, quotation.

- Design specific, unique assignments (not the generic research paper or personal narrative).
- Invite conversation and questions about the assignment; acknowledge the challenges students may face as they complete it. (Intentional plagiarism is often a result of students' feeling overwhelmed.)
- Negotiate specific projects, informed by writers' goals, within general guidelines.
- Ask writers to collect specific artifacts or conduct their own observational research in addition to secondary research.
- Have writers join local conversations.
- Encourage writers to use their own experiences and perspectives as sources of information and evidence in their projects.
- Incorporate regular in-class writing.
- Read multiple drafts throughout writers' writing process (but don't feel the need to respond to or grade everything).
- Ask for author's notes in which writers explain their choices.
- Incorporate frequent peer response groups.
- Have writers compose revision plans.

Of course, all the teaching strategies in the world will not guarantee that students won't plagiarize. But we can minimize plagiarism by making it an explicit part of our instruction, by providing students resources for understanding what it is and how to avoid it, and above all, by offering them meaningful writing projects.

In addition to a good writing handbook, we recommend that students be directed to the following online resources on plagiarism:

- Indiana University Writing Tutorial Services: http://www.indiana.edu/~wts/pamphlets/plagiarism.shtml
- Purdue University Online Writing Lab: http://owl.english.purdue.edu/handouts/research/r_plagiar.html
- Northwestern University Academic Integrity: http://www.northwestern.edu/uacc/plagiar.html

Using Quotations Effectively

One of the most important and difficult skills associated with research is effectively incorporating others' ideas and words into our own writing. Learning *how* to use quotations begins with careful consideration of *why* and *when* to use them. (We have all encountered student—and sometimes "professional"—writing in which quotations seem "dropped in," arbitrarily placed within the author's own text. In the former case, this is often a function of students' trying to meet a minimum requirement for quotations or citations.) So it is important to discuss with students the uses of quotation:

- Giving credit to the source of an idea or argument
- Giving voice to a particularly useful or insightful framing of an idea or argument (i.e., when there is something special in the way an author expresses that idea or argument)
- Lending credibility to one's own ideas or arguments by calling on a recognized authority

In each case, the point is that writers are *in conversation* with other writers. Just as in a productive and enjoyable face-to-face conversation, writers attempt to weave their own ideas seamlessly with those of others. This of course takes a good deal of practice. Students will need help introducing and following up on quotations in the context of their own unfolding ideas and arguments.

After students write their drafts, you might have them highlight places in their texts where they use quotations and either individually or in groups ask themselves questions such as these:

- Is it clear why the quotation is being used? Is it relevant to and does it help develop the discussion of the piece?
- Is the quotation clearly and smoothly introduced? Is the reader prepared for it?
- Does the writer provide enough information about the source of the quotation? If the author or the speaker of the source is an expert, is that made clear?
- Is the quotation followed up on and woven into the piece?

We can also have students ask these questions of published writers by having them examine why and how practicing writers do this work. The key to this activity, like so many of the activities in this book, is to help our students reflect carefully on the choices writers make.

Chapter 9

A Writer's Process Toolbox

The tools collected here are intended to help students as they undertake any writing project and are not specific to any particular kind or form of writing. We have organized them according to different "stages" of the writing process: invention (or getting started), drafting, revising, and editing. But note that writing rarely happens in such a linear way. Our own processes are often messy, unpredictable, and recursive. We sometimes turn to "invention" tools—which are designed to help us get started—when we are in the middle of a draft, or even between drafts. Or when we think we're almost ready for a final editing session, we find we must go back and revise a major idea. This might even lead us back to drafting, if we find ourselves onto an entirely new idea. So we invite you and your students to use whatever tools might serve your purpose at any given time.

Throughout this chapter, you will find sidebars intended to enrich your consideration and use of these tools. In Chapter 10, "A Teacher's Toolbox," you'll find elaborations on much of the sidebar material.

General Process Advice

- **Set clear goals and expectations with students for each project.** Writers do their best work when they understand the task at hand and when that task and its consequences are meaningful and beneficial to them. Talk with students about why you're asking them to complete the project and what you hope they will learn from it. The project toolboxes will help you formulate these rationales.

- **Help students self-assess.** The most important function of assessment is to help students self-assess: to come to know themselves as writers and learners. Some of the tools below, including writer's notes and revision plans, will help your students do this work.

- **Help students attend to project maintenance.** Real-life writing projects put different demands on teachers and writers than do traditional connect-the-dots writing assignments that can be completed quickly and easily. Young writers will need help setting reasonable goals, breaking projects down into "doable" chunks, locating and using resources (including each other), developing workable timelines, and so on. While it is tempting to do all this for young writers, we strongly advise that you allow your students to make at least some choices in mapping out their work. Some deadlines are of course necessary, but all writers must learn how to manage their projects; as teachers, we can find low-risk, high-yield ways to put some parts of the writing process into students' hands.

- **Require students to generate at least two drafts of their projects, preferably more.** Despite persistent myths about "inspired" writers who spit out pristine first drafts, writers of all stripes need opportunities to try out ideas, to shape their meanings, to develop their purposes and audiences, to learn the conventions of genre, and so on. We sometimes ask students to produce deliberately messy first attempts to get ideas on paper. This strategy is often useful to struggling writers. But shaping our ideas and our prose across multiple drafts is important for all writers.

- **Treat revision as re-vision: seeing again.** It is important that young writers learn that effective revision is not about "fixing" a text—that is, editing, or proofreading. Effective revision is about discovering and shaping—or reshaping—meaning. Even if students are pleased with their first or second drafts, encourage them to go back to them after some time elapses, with fresh eyes and fresh perspectives, recognizing that not only the words, sentences, and punctuation may need more work, but also the ideas themselves. (See Chapter 4 for more on the concept of re-vision.)

- **Provide students with various kinds of teacher and peer feedback throughout their writing process.** It is important to be mindful of the different kinds of information students need at different parts of the writing process, from brainstorming sessions and conferences in which they can bounce ideas off of others to substantive written responses on first drafts to more focused, evaluative response to final drafts. Too much evaluative feedback early on in the writing process can stifle writers, for example, while too much formative feedback later in the process can overwhelm them.

Invention Tools (Getting Started)

In this section, you will find tools designed to help your students generate ideas to write about and to shape their early ideas about their writing projects (see Activities 9-1 through 9-5).

Activity 9-1
Brainstorming, Freewriting, and Focused Freewriting

Brainstorming

1. Write the numbers 1 through 20 on the left side of a notebook page.
2. Now list 20 topics you might want to write about. Don't think! Just write whatever comes into your head, no matter how ridiculous or off-topic it seems. There will be time later to shape and categorize; the point of brainstorming is to delay that work in the hope that this freedom will generate some creative thinking. Don't stop until you reach 20. ➜

Freewriting

(Based on Peter Elbow, Writing Without Teachers, *1973)*

1. Find a quiet spot where you won't be interrupted. And make sure you have access to a clock or watch.

2. Now, write for five (or, if you're ambitious, ten) minutes. Don't think, and don't stop! The only rule is that the pen cannot leave the page, and it must keep moving. If you get stuck, just write nonsense, or "I'm stuck I'm stuck I'm stuck" until you become unstuck. Just write whatever's in your head: ideas, questions, song lyrics, and so on.

Focused Freewriting

1. Find a quiet spot where you won't be interrupted. And make sure you have access to a clock or watch.

2. At the top of a blank page, write the topic or idea you want to write about. It could be a single word—*school, family, religion, music*—or it could be a prompt such as "Where I'm From," "My Name," or "A Breakthrough Moment."

3. Now, write for five (or, if you're ambitious, ten) minutes. When you get stuck, reread your topic/prompt and begin again. Keep writing nonstop until time has elapsed. Don't censor yourself; the point is to turn off your internal editor.

Teaching Writing That Matters © 2008 by Chris W. Gallagher and Amy Lee, Scholastic Professional.

Activity 9-2

Lifeline

1. Turn a piece of notebook paper sideways and draw a line from left to right. (You may want to use a bigger piece of paper, if available.) This line represents your lifetime, from when you were born (left) to the present (right).

2. Mark off important segments of your life. You could divide the timeline using your schooling—preschool, elementary, middle or junior high, high ➡

school, college—or by some other set of events: where you lived, for example, or jobs you've held. How we divide our timelines can often tell us a lot about what's important to us.

3. Now, fill in the timeline, moving segment by segment. Try to remember as many events, people, places, objects, and experiences as you can. You can write some key words on the timeline, or you can draw images.

4. When you are ready to do some writing, choose a moment on your timeline and freewrite about it. Why is it important? What meaning does it hold for you? What would you want other people to know about it?

Activity 9-3

Mapping Your Place

1. Grab some paper (preferably newsprint-sized sheets) and some markers.

2. You'll be drawing a map that represents the trajectory of your life. Begin with the outline. What shape should your map take? Should it look like your hometown, your state, the United States? Or should it have a metaphorical shape: a ladder, a set of steps, a set of concentric circles?

3. Now, start placing the "coordinates" on your map: the big events, people, places, and so on. These could be symbolic: a church to represent your faith, for instance. Or they could be straightforward: a picture of your childhood home. Also feel free to use key words—though you should try to focus on visual representation.

4. When your map is complete and you are ready to write, simply choose an item on the map and freewrite about it. Why is it important? What meaning does it hold for you? What would you want other people to know about it? And so on.

(Based on ideas explored in R. Brooke and J. McIntosh, "Deep Maps," 2007)

Activity 9-4
Authority Lists

1. Make lists of the following:
   - Skills you have that not everyone has
   - Hobbies you have that not everyone has
   - Things you've taught to others
   - Things you know that not everyone knows
   - Places you've visited or things you've witnessed that not everyone has
   - People you know whom others might like to know about
2. When you're ready to write, choose an item on one of your lists and do some freewriting about it. What's special about this expertise? Who might be interested in hearing about it?

Teaching Writing That Matters © 2008 by Chris W. Gallagher and Amy Lee, Scholastic Professional.

Activity 9-5
Inquiry Lists

1. Make lists of the following:
   - Skills you don't have but wish you did
   - Hobbies you wish you knew more about
   - Things others teach that you'd like to learn
   - Things others know that you'd like to know
   - Places others have visited or things they've witnessed that you'd like to see as well
   - People you don't know but wish you did
2. When you're ready to write, choose an item on one of your lists and do some freewriting about it. Why are you interested in it? How could you learn more? How could you design a writing project that would allow you to learn more, and to share what you learn with others?

Teaching Writing That Matters © 2008 by Chris W. Gallagher and Amy Lee, Scholastic Professional.

Drafting Tools

In this section, you will find tools designed to help your students flesh out their ideas and develop more extensive drafts (see Activities 9-6 through 9-8).

The following activity may be adapted for purposes such as focusing on specific details in fiction or poetry writing or focusing on a single source, passage in a source, or idea in several sources while writing with research.

Activity 9-6
One-Inch Picture Frame

1. Think about an experience you have had; visualize it from beginning to end: the what, who, when, why, where. Or, if you're planning to draft a response, position, or argument, think through the big picture. Who is involved? What is at stake? Why does it matter? What perspectives or other voices come into play?

2. Now, pretend you have a one-inch frame that you move around on that experience or idea. Maybe you move it to cover a single person or a single detail such as the table where you were sitting when something happened. Perhaps you move the frame to cover one supporting idea within your larger position, or to home in on one important voice or text in the larger conversation about the issue. Find the small moment inside the entire experience or argument that seems especially significant or meaningful to you in some way.

3. Now, write about just that moment or idea. Forget about all the things you're not writing about and just focus on the one or two things in the picture frame. Think and write in a very detailed way about what is in the frame. Generate around 300 words (a little over a typed page). Try writing until you've covered everything in the frame.

4. If this strategy works for you, move the frame to another piece of the experience or idea and write about what shows up there.

(Adapted from Anne Lamott, Bird by Bird, *1994, and an activity designed by Rochelle Harris)*

Activity 9-7
Looping

1. Read your notes or the freewriting you've done so far. Underline an idea or image or even just a phrase that intrigues or surprises you.
2. Write your underlined phrase or sentence or paragraph on a fresh sheet of paper and use it to begin a focused freewrite.
3. Repeat this process two or three times, always beginning your focused freewrite with something you've taken from the previous freewrite.
4. Once you complete this process, it may be wise to let the writing sit for a bit. When you do return to it, see what connections you can draw as you reread. Any patterns or trends? Can you see yourself looping toward any ideas in particular? Looping away from others? What can this tool teach you about where your interest or passion really is? What writing, or what ideas, can you keep as you push your piece forward into a draft?

(Adapted from Peter Elbow, "Loop Writing," in Writing With Power, *1998)*

Activity 9-8
Possibility Statements

1. Reread your notes or early draftwork.
2. Complete the following statements:

    *   As a _____, I am concerned about/interested in _____ .
                                                              topic
    *   After experiencing/learning about _____, I am concerned

        about/interested in _____ .
                            topic
    *   Now, I could write a/an _____ to _____ in order to _____.
                                genre/form   audience   purpose

➡

Getting and Giving Effective Peer Response

In this section, you will find tools designed to help your students receive and offer effective peer response (Activities 9-9 through 9-11) as well as some guidelines for establishing and facilitating peer response groups.

General Template for Peer Response Groups

Each writer brings a short piece of writing to share with two or three peers.

1. Teacher will call out time to ensure equal attention to each student's draft. (Alternatively, a timekeeper may be chosen for each group.)
2. A bold volunteer reads her draft aloud to the group. (If possible, copies of the draft are distributed.) The writer does *not* apologize for the quality of her draft; these are drafts!
3. When this person finishes reading, the others take a moment to gather their thoughts and perhaps jot down a few notes to shape their comments. Then they share their thoughts. The writer takes part in a dialogue with responders until the teacher or time-keeper signals that it is time to move on.

4. This process is repeated until each person in the group has shared his or her draft and received response.

Activity 9-9
Writer's Notes

1. Reread your draft.
2. Draft a one- or two-paragraph note that does the following:
   - Explains, briefly, where you are with the piece (this is a loose first draft—freewriting, really; I've revised twice, and I think it's almost ready to send)
   - Tells readers what you're trying to do with the piece (I'm trying to capture this experience for someone who has little context for it; I want to convince a hostile audience that this idea is worth considering)
   - Asks readers for a certain kind of reading (e.g., I could use a lot of sayback [tell me what you think I'm saying] so I can see what I have through somebody else's eyes; handle with care because this is really raw to me; rip it apart—I need an aggressive, "doubting" reading; help me see what the counterarguments would be)
   - Provides some questions that help readers understand what you need/want from them. (Where does the argument seem thin? How can I better develop this character? Are there places where you are confused? Is an administrator likely to find this case compelling?)

Teaching Writing That Matters © 2008 by Chris W. Gallagher and Amy Lee, Scholastic Professional.

Activity 9-10

Examples of Effective and Ineffective Peer Response

Your job, as a responder, is to provide the writer with feedback on a draft. Since you'll be giving response to a piece-in-progress, your aim is to give the writer some ideas for when she goes home again to think about and work on turning this into the next draft. You are an experienced reader. You know when something is working to pull you in, convince you, teach you. You also know when a text is missing something, when there is a leap in logic or structure, when you can't follow something, or aren't quite convinced by it. The trick will be to learn why these moments occur in a text (the effective and the not-so-effective). So you'll have no trouble identifying them, but you might need to work on how to turn this into useful feedback for the writer. Following are some examples of ineffective and effective feedback.

Ineffective Feedback

"I really like your essay. I think it's great. I had a similar experience so I know what you mean. I enjoyed this a lot. Good work. Keep it up."

> *Discussion:* How will the writer know why it's great or how to make it greater? These are all drafts, and every piece of writing improves with revision. This writer won't have any idea what is making this piece effective to this reader. She knows the piece seems to be working, but not why. Or maybe she just will think the reader was a little lazy and didn't take the time to really read the piece carefully and thoughtfully.

Effective Feedback

"Your essay is great. The way you use specific examples all the time to explain your point is effective—like when you're trying to explain how you felt ➜

after the experience and you compare your feelings to a washing machine (5th paragraph). I had a similar experience, but hadn't put it into words really and seeing you do it helps me understand my own experience better. It's really good when you talk to us directly, instead of talking at some strangers. This makes me feel from the beginning as though I am in the piece, the memory, with you—as though you're talking to me."

> *Discussion: Here, the reader is providing specific examples about what worked for her in the essay. She doesn't just comment vaguely and generally on the essay from a distance. Instead, she points to specific moments in the piece and explains why they worked for her. She gives the writer a much better sense of what's working and why.*

Ineffective Feedback

"I was pretty confused the whole time. What was your point? You jump around all the time and I can't follow the ideas. This needs a lot of structure and better organization."

> *Discussion: The writer won't know why the piece was confusing, where it was confusing, or what to do to remedy the problem. The writer might again not even be sure whether the reader gave this piece a careful review, given how vague and general the critique is.*

Effective Feedback

"I found your essay to be pretty confusing—I think because I was never really sure what the central point was. Is your main focus how teachers are part of the problem you describe because they don't give individual attention to students and are too concerned with covering all the material (as you suggest at the end)? Or is it that schools need to do a better job supporting teachers so they can do their job (which you say at the beginning)? Sometimes, I wasn't sure ➜

Teaching Writing That Matters

whether you were describing and defining the problem or calling for a change in order to address the problem. For instance, on page 2, when you begin describing that history class you took. Also, I think the piece is confusing because sometimes I wasn't sure I understood some of the transitions. See my margin comments on pages 1, 2. In these places, you lost me. I think if you rearrange things, focus first on defining the problem and then move on to addressing it, we could follow you better."

Discussion: Here, the writer has a much clearer sense of where the essay breaks down for the reader and why. The reader is offering specific examples, and also is providing some suggestions for revising to remedy the problems.

Teaching Writing That Matters © 2008 by Chris W. Gallagher and Amy Lee, Scholastic Professional.

Advice for Facilitating Peer Response

- Explain purposes of response groups: to give/get revision advice, to learn from each other, to learn how to talk about writing, to improve critical-reading skills.
- Practice as a whole class, perhaps on a piece of your own writing.
- Establish a reliable but flexible procedure.
- Be patient (students need time, practice, and shared language to do this work).
- Ask students to make use of writer's notes.
- Keep time; ensure all drafts receive roughly equal attention.
- Monitor groups, gather student feedback about their functioning, and determine when/if to change them.

Activity 9-11
Response Strategies

Here are some strategies you can use when you are responding to each other's writing:

- Summarizing/saying back (Here's what I see this saying . . .)
- Glossing (Here's a word or phrase that condenses this paragraph or section . . .)
- Responding (As I read this paragraph, I . . .)
- Pointing (What seems most important here is . . .) (What seems to be missing here is . . .)
- Extending (You could also apply this to . . .) (What would happen if you . . .)
- Encouraging (This section works well for me because . . .)
- Suggesting (If I were you, I would add that . . .) (You could move that paragraph . . .)
- Soliciting (Could you say more here about . . .)
- Connecting (In my experience, this . . .) (That's like what X says . . .) (I saw some research on this . . .)
- Evaluating (This opening is focused, well-developed, and catchy . . .)
- Arguing (Another way to look at this is . . .)
- Questioning (Why do you say . . . ?) (What does this part mean?)

Teaching Writing That Matters © 2008 by Chris W. Gallagher and Amy Lee, Scholastic Professional.

Revision Tools

In this section, you will find tools (Activities 9-12 and 9-13) that will help your students read their own drafts for possibilities and revise their ideas, not just the words on the page.

Activity 9-12
Hot-Spotting

1. Choose a draft you'd like to develop. Reread the draft, marking (underline, highlight, star) places where you think your writing is working. This could be a sentence that expresses a thought-provoking idea, a strong or startling image, a central tension, or a place that could be explored in more detail. These places are the "hot spots" of your draft.

2. Copy one of these hot spots onto the top of a clean page; then, put your draft aside. (If you are working on a computer, copy the passage and paste it to a new document.) If the passage is long, you can cut it out of the original or fold the draft so only the hot spot shows.

3. Now write, using the hot spot as a new first sentence (or paragraph). Write for 15 to 20 minutes, or however long you need to develop your ideas. Don't worry if you "lose" your original idea. You might be in the process of finding a better one.

4. Repeat the process as often as feels right.

5. Now put your piece back together. You might want to just add the new writing into the piece or substitute it for something you can now delete. You might even take out large sections of the original writing and reorganize the rest around your new writing. Consider how your conception of the "whole" of this draft changes with the new material.

6. In your writer's notes or revision plan, focus on two things:

    (a) Write some directions for what you want to do with this writing the next time you work on it. What do you have to change about the text to include the new writing?

    (b) Reflect upon your revision process. What did you learn about your topic/text from this process? Did you pursue a tangential idea? Deepen or extend an original idea? Change your perspective on the topic? Realize that you are really interested in another topic altogether?

Teaching Writing That Matters © 2008 by Chris W. Gallagher and Amy Lee, Scholastic Professional.

Activity 9-13
Revision Plan

Read your draft. Try to read not only for what *is* in the draft, but also for what *isn't*—what could be. Read, that is, for possibilities. (Some writers like to read their drafts twice: once for strengths and once for possibilities.)

Write a paragraph or two in which you answer these questions:

- What strengths do you see in the draft, and how do you plan to preserve or enhance those strengths?
- What possibilities do you see for your draft now, and which might you want to try out? How might you do that work?
- What questions or problems linger in your draft, and how do you plan to address them?
- How will you refine, expand, or otherwise revise this piece?
- What kind of help might you need to make these changes? Would getting feedback help? Finding a text that does similar work? Just making the time?
- What will your process be for doing this work? When and how will you make the changes you're considering?

Teaching Writing That Matters © 2008 by Chris W. Gallagher and Amy Lee, Scholastic Professional.

Editing Tools

This section provides tools that will help your students polish their final drafts (Activity 9-14) as well as tips for responding to student drafts.

Teaching Writing That Matters

Three Editing Tools

Reading Backward

With a pen or pencil in your hand and a hard copy of your draft in front of you, read the last sentence of the piece. Make any necessary grammatical, spelling, or usage corrections. Now read the sentence before that. Correct again. Continue with this process until you've reached the beginning of your draft. (The idea here is that when we read our own drafts, we often "see" in them what we intended to write, rather than what is actually on the page. Reading backward forces us out of the rhythm of our writing. This tool is useful for near-final drafts.)

Round-Robin Editing Session

1. Get into small groups (four or five members).
2. Each person passes his or her draft to the person on the right.
3. Each person edits/corrects the draft he or she has been handed. Work quickly; do not comment on the draft; just make any corrections you think are necessary.
4. When the teacher calls time, pass again to the right and edit/correct.
5. This process is continued until drafts are returned to their writers.

Reading Table

1. Everyone places his or her draft on a table or desk at the center of the room.
2. Everyone chooses a draft at random and returns with it to his or her seat.
3. Read and comment on the draft. You may or may not identify yourself as a responder. When you are done commenting, return the draft to the reading table and take another.
4. Repeat this process for the allotted time.
5. At the end of the session, writers pick up their drafts.

Teaching Writing That Matters © 2008 by Chris W. Gallagher and Amy Lee, Scholastic Professional.

Tips for Teacher Response

1. Respond as a *reader*, not just a teacher/evaluator. For example, instead of scrawling "idea underdeveloped" in the margin, try "I'd like to hear more about this," or "Can you say more about this idea?" Or, instead of "awkward construction," try "I'm having a hard time following this sentence."

2. Consider where students are in their writing process. Do they need ideas to write about, ways to develop their ideas, other ways of looking at their topic, support for their research, strategies for shaping their material, editing help?

3. Create a *context* for your comments. Make sure students understand that all of your responses are offered in the spirit of support, even when some of the commentary is critical.

4. Respond to writer's notes. Response is a way to be in conversation with writers; responding to writer's notes honors their own ideas about and goals for their writing.

5. Aim for "just enough." Too little response leaves students without adequate guidance and often with the impression that we do not care about their writing. Too much response leaves them overwhelmed and unable to identify and focus on the most important features of their work. Typically, an occasional marginal comment and a substantive but not terribly lengthy end-comment is "just enough" for a solid draft.

6. Most important: keep them writing. Our overarching goal, whenever we respond, should be to help students *want* to keep working on their writing.

Self-Assessment Tools

Many of the tools in the previous sections—including writer's notes and revision plans—ask students to self-assess; this section presents a couple of larger, more sustained reflection tools (Activities 9-15 and 9-16).

Activity 9-15
Project Learning Letter

1. Reread all the drafts for this project.
2. Write a short (one-page) letter to me that answers the following questions:
   - What were your goals for this project?
   - What have you been able to accomplish with this project? Have you met your goals?
   - What have been your challenges as a writer/reader/learner during this project? Where has your writing fallen short of your expectations? How can you work on this?
   - What have you learned about yourself as a writer during this project? How will this change how or what you write?
   - What are your writing goals now? Have they changed or developed as a result of this project? What will you work on next?

Teaching Writing That Matters © 2008 by Chris W. Gallagher and Amy Lee, Scholastic Professional.

Activity 9-16
Portfolio

A portfolio is a collection of your work over time. But it is much more than just a folder of individual pieces. It is a picture of who you are and what you can do as a writer. You will be building your portfolio throughout the term, so be sure to *keep all drafts of your work* in a folder or binder.

At the end of the term, you will choose three examples of your very best work. You will include all drafts, including writer's notes and your final, polished version. Your portfolio will consist of these projects as well as an introduction that does the following: ➜

1. Explains why you chose these three pieces and what you think are the strengths of each one.
2. Discusses what you learned about yourself as a writer this term. Be sure to explain *how* you learned this, including what supported that learning.
3. Describes any challenges you faced as a writer this semester and how (or whether) you overcame them.
4. Explains what your writing goals were for the semester and how well you think you have accomplished them.
5. Reflects on what your writing goals are now, as you move on from the course, and how you intend to pursue them.

Teaching Writing That Matters © 2008 by Chris W. Gallagher and Amy Lee, Scholastic Professional.

Benefits of Portfolios

- They capture writers' development over time.
- They demonstrate how students work across different purposes, audiences, and contexts.
- They represent students' writing processes, as well as their products.
- They encourage student reflection on their own work.
- They are a comprehensive tool for writing assessment and are tied to classroom instruction.

Selected Bibliography on Writing Portfolios

Belanoff, P., & Dickson, M. (1991). *Portfolios: Process and product.* Portsmouth, NH: Heinemann-Boynton/Cook.

Black, L., Daiker, D. A., Sommers, J., & Stygall, G. (Eds.). (1994). *New directions in portfolio assessment: Reflective practice, critical theory, and large-scale scoring.* Portsmouth, NH: Heinemann-Boynton/Cook.

Cooper, C. R., & Odell, L. (Eds.). (1999). *Evaluating writing: The role of teachers' knowledge about text, learning, and culture.* Urbana, IL: National Council of Teachers of English.

Graves, D., & Sunstein, B. (Eds.). (1992). *Portfolio portraits.* Portsmouth, NH: Heinemann.

Murphy, S., & Smith, M. (2001). *Writing portfolios.* Portsmouth, NH: Heinemann.

Yancey, K. B., & Weiser, I. (Eds.). (1997). *Situating portfolios: Four perspectives.* Logan, UT: Utah State University Press.

Chapter 10

A Teacher's Toolbox

The tools collected here may be used by individual teachers or by groups of teachers working together in professional learning communities, inquiry groups, or staff meetings. Whereas the tools in the writer's process toolbox are intended to help your students develop their writing, the tools in this teacher's toolbox are intended to help you develop your teaching of writing.

As we did in the writer's process toolbox (Chapter 9), we want to stress that tools alone are never enough; it's only when thoughtful builders use them in appropriate, effective ways that tools become useful and meaningful. Likewise, just as there is no One Right Way to write, there is no One Right Way to teach. "Good teaching" is as complicated and context-bound a concept as "good writing." So our intent here is not to offer fail-proof formulas or silver bullets. Instead, it's to provide you with a set of tools that will help you develop as what we've called a "reflective practitioner."

Reflective practice, recall, is at the very heart of teaching and writing. It is an ongoing activity that involves creativity, self-awareness, and thoughtful planning. In simplest terms, reflective practice is the act of connecting *what* we are doing with *why* we are doing it.

So our hope is to help you develop a teaching framework that guides your decision making as a teacher. This framework includes beliefs and knowledge about effective teaching and writing. It is the source of our rationales for what we do. Without it, choosing what to do in the classroom is like choosing a recipe: if it looks like it will "work," we try it. This is an impoverished criterion for making teaching choices. A better criterion is that we know or have reason to believe that a certain activity or classroom focus will promote student learning. For instance, for us, asking students to revise their writing is crucial because we believe the ability to enter into a text or an idea in order to re-see it, to re-imagine its possibilities, is a key to writing (and thinking) development.

To be sure, this framework is tentative and evolving, even for very experienced teachers. The trick, it seems to us, is to do our best to operate from our deeply held beliefs and our professional knowledge without allowing ourselves to slip into dogma or dead routine. To do this, we need to shuttle back and forth between our ideas and beliefs on the one hand and the lived experience of our classrooms on the other. Our teaching philosophy should put pressure on our teaching practice, but so too should our teaching practice put pressure back on our teaching philosophy.

Think of this toolbox, then, as supplemental to the reflective activities for teachers in Part II of this book. (Indeed, some of these tools are alternative or extended versions of shorter activities found in those chapters.) We invite you, either alone or with colleagues, to find tools that will suit your purposes. We have organized the tools into the following categories:

Reflecting on practice: We begin with some general discussion of reflective practice, including some of the obstacles you might face in your teaching community or institutional context. We also discuss some of the supports you can seek out or create in order to promote your continued development as a reflective teacher. Finally, we provide prompts for composing a statement of teaching philosophy and a teaching portfolio.

Guiding effective peer response: In this section, we provide guidelines for and examples of facilitating effective peer response to help you engage your students in this work. We also provide templates for organizing and focusing small peer response groups and whole-class "workshopping."

Responding to and assessing student writing: In this section, we consider the range of occasions for and means of responding to and assessing student writing. We discuss choices about when, how, and why to respond. This section also highlights rubrics and portfolios.

Using readings to teach writing: In this section, we discuss the challenges of fostering engaged responses to readings and the importance of being specific about the kinds of work we ask students to do with texts. We discuss, in particular, rhetorical reading or reading as a writer and offer some sample assignments aimed at generating this type of engaged response.

Reflecting on Practice: Obstacles and Supports

Before you read this section, think about what hinders or facilitates your ability to do your best teaching. List as many obstacles and supports as you can.

Now consider what hinders or facilitates your ability to reflect well and deeply on your teaching. List as many obstacles and supports as you can. ❖

In our work with new and experienced teachers, we have encountered four common obstacles to reflective practice. As teachers and members of teaching communities, we need to be on guard against these obstacles, and to develop supports to help us overcome them.

Obstacle: Lack of Time

This is hands-down the most commonly cited obstacle to reflective practice. Who has time to do all this reflective work? It takes time to reflect deeply and well on our practice. It's easier (because quicker) to bypass it and go with "what works," relying on what led to auspicious results in the past (or for other people).

Supports

Alas, we have no magic bullet here. There are no shortcuts to becoming a reflective practitioner. However, we would make three points. First, as we argue in Chapter 1, we need to refuse the idea that reflection is a luxury. Reflection is integral to teaching and learning. We simply must make time for it. Certainly, time management is crucial, and so is balancing teaching responsibilities with other professional and personal responsibilities. We must set parameters around our work as teachers, or else it will take over our lives (especially for those of us who love the work). But we should never forget that the success of our students depends in large part on our willingness and ability to be fully present for them, and this requires us to take care of ourselves.

Second, consider all of the "professional development" time that is wasted on talking heads and irrelevant meetings. Fortunately, professional development in many districts is moving in the direction of embedded, team-based, discussion-oriented structures such as professional learning communities, action research projects, and inquiry groups (see Gallagher, 2007). We hope this trend continues and that districts make time for and reward teachers' individual and collective reflection on their work. This mindset shift—from the notion that teachers should "sit-n-git" from experts to the idea that teachers *are* experts who can teach each other—is a potentially powerful support for reflective practice and will allow teachers to make much better use of the time available to them within their contracted hours.

Third, while there's no denying that reflective practice takes significant time and effort, it's also true that reflective practitioners we know are far more satisfied with their work and tend not to "burn out." The key support here is reflective practice itself, because it is an engine of renewal. In this sense, we see a considerable "saved cost." Think of the teachers you know who are disengaged and simply going through the motions. Aren't they marking time? Doesn't time seem to move awfully slowly for them?

Obstacle: Damage-Control Mode

This obstacle is common among new teachers, who are understandably anxious about their professional responsibilities and often spend a great deal of time imagining all the possible scenarios in which *things might go wrong*. They picture unruly students, offensive texts, activities that fall flat, discussions that won't take off, and all manner of teacherly incompetence. They worry incessantly about making mistakes and, frankly, about not being liked by their students. Sometimes before class starts or perhaps at the first sign that the classroom will not be the hoped-for utopia, the teacher moves into damage-control mode. She casts about for "failproof" strategies, which often turn out to be strategies of containment. To ensure students aren't offended by one another's writing, she institutes a policy outlawing all kinds of inappropriate language or topics. To avoid student silence, he requires everyone to talk every day. These are not *necessarily* "bad" practices, and we would consider using them under certain circumstances, but our point is that in these scenarios, they are designed to control for negative possibilities that the teacher cannot predict. And when the teacher makes enough of these moves, she has built an approach to teaching on the basis of self-preservation, rather than her beliefs and knowledge about what helps students learn. This is perhaps understandable, but it is not professionally responsible.

Supports

Some anxiety is unavoidable, for new and experienced teachers alike. In fact, we believe anxiety is often *good*: it is, after all, a form of excitement and one index of commitment (if we didn't care about what we were doing, we wouldn't get nervous about it). But while our nervousness doesn't fully go away over the course of the semester, nor should it drive our teaching.

The keys to avoiding damage-control mode are humility and charity. By humility, we mean a self-conscious awareness that we and our students sometimes will make bad choices, and that this is a risk we must be willing to take for the sake of students' learning. We cannot expect to be perfect teachers in a perfect classroom; beyond being unrealistic, this expectation is actually damaging, as we suggest above. Instead, we need to be humble and patient enough to take risks and to make mistakes. Just as writers must make mistakes in order to grow, so must teachers.

By charity, we mean that teachers do their best work when they operate from the premise that students are good people trying to do good work. Some students may *prove* otherwise, but it is ungenerous and unwise for us to *assume* otherwise. We believe that effective teachers always respect their students and their abilities, and that respect entails viewing each student as an asset to the classroom, not a liability. As bell hooks (1994) writes in *Teaching to Transgress*, "The bottom-line assumption has to be that everyone in the classroom is able to act responsibly" (p. 152). To teach students is to take them seriously as complex human beings with ideas, investments, values, and skills worthy of careful consideration.

Obstacle: Isolation

Another obstacle to reflective practice for new and experienced teachers arises from conceptions of teaching as a private, individual affair. Traditionally, teaching happens behind a closed door; it is a private space over which the individual teacher has total control. While we believe deeply in intellectual freedom, we don't believe it requires this kind of isolation, which is a recipe for stagnation. Without ongoing professional conversations and encouragement, teachers tend to rely on the familiar and they fall into passionless routines.

Supports

Reflective practice requires continual renewal. Sources of renewal include a supportive local teaching community (fellow teachers with shared interests and commitments) and professional resources (including teachers elsewhere, the literature on teaching writing, and professional organizations such as the National Council of Teachers of English and the National Writing Project). Some teachers are blessed with an existing teaching community in their schools. Others must create such a community, seeking out teachers with whom to converse about teaching (perhaps using this book to guide these conversations!). In either case, a supportive but challenging teaching community serves several purposes: it provides encouragement and moral support; it provides a space to share ideas and resources; it helps teachers engage in problem solving; and it offers feedback on teachers' developing ideas. In whatever form it takes, it functions much as a writing group does for writers.

Obstacle: Complacency

Finally, perhaps the most serious obstacle to reflective practice is a sense that one's teaching is "good enough," that no further development is required. This is fairly common among experienced teachers who have fallen into routines. (But we also know wonderful longtime teachers who are never complacent, but rather relentlessly unquiet.) However understandable given the strains of a teaching life, complacency is antithetical to engaging teaching.

Supports

This may come as cold comfort to new teachers who hope things will "settle down" once they get a little experience, but the fact is, the best teachers we know never do settle down. To be sure, they typically have a stable framework for their teaching; but this does not translate into routinized practice. Why? Because these teachers operate from a commitment to their work. The antidote to complacency is *passion*. And passion, incidentally, is contagious—if we find passion in our teaching community, in our professional resources, and in our students, we are more likely to find it in ourselves. All of the supports mentioned in this section serve as a buttress against complacency.

Statement of Teaching Philosophy

Draft a short statement—one or two pages—that articulates your guiding beliefs about teaching writing. (Note: The "This I Believe About Teaching" activity in Chapter 3 is an excellent exercise to try before drafting your statement.) No two statements of teaching philosophy are exactly alike, but effective statements have these common elements:

- A central idea, belief, commitment, or goal (sometimes expressed through a metaphor)
- A small number of corollary ideas, beliefs, commitments, or goals
- A description of what the teacher thinks, why the teacher thinks it, and how the ideas, beliefs, commitments, or goals play out in the classroom
- Examples, typically drawn from classrooms
- An engaging voice that tells us something about who the person is as a teacher

Teaching Portfolio

In order to develop a teaching portfolio, you will collect, select, and reflect on a variety of teaching artifacts over time—a semester, a year, several years—presenting a rich portrait of yourself as a teacher of writing and of your teaching practice. Think of a teaching portfolio as a text made up of other texts. In other words, it should be greater than the sum of its parts, more than simply a folder of "stuff." Portfolio designers must be thoughtful about what they choose to include and how they frame each artifact as part of that larger portrait. What does each artifact suggest about the teacher or his or her teaching? How does it connect with other artifacts in the portfolio?

Start with a binder or a folder with pockets. (Some teachers like to decorate their portfolios.) Using your Statement of Teaching Philosophy and/or your "This I Believe" essay to guide your thinking, begin collecting artifacts that you believe represent something important about your teaching practice or who you are as a teacher of writing. These could include classroom materials you've developed, student evaluations, supervisor evaluations, information on special projects you've participated in (including curriculum revision, action research, and the like), examples of student work at various levels, results of student assessments, letters of recommendation, photographs, a list of honors and awards—and the list goes on. Be sure to include your Statement of Teaching Philosophy and/or "This I Believe" essay as well as a statement that explains your teaching responsibilities.

For each artifact, write a short note that explains what the artifact is and why you have chosen it—in other words, what you think it demonstrates about your teaching. When you have several artifacts, think about how you might organize them. Does the order of presentation matter? Do you see themes across the artifacts? Would it make sense to organize the portfolio by theme or by kind of text (lesson plans, responses to student writing, assignments, etc.)? Be creative: the organization of the portfolio might say something important about you or your teaching. Now, step back from the artifacts and write a one- to three-page cover letter for the portfolio highlighting for your readers—your future self, colleagues, a supervisor, a prospective employer—what you most want them to know about your teaching. Direct readers to specific places in the portfolio; show them your best, most interesting work.

Teaching Writing That Matters

Guiding Effective Peer Response: Small Groups and Whole-Class Workshops

Peer response is a staple of Writing Studies classrooms because it is a staple of all writing communities, whether we're talking about academic disciplines, publishing collectives, bloggers, or informal writing groups. In these communities, writers share their work not only to get revision suggestions—although that is of course important—but also because reading others' work is valuable in and of itself. For this reason, it is important to stress with students that peer response is about both writing and reading.

There are many ways to structure peer response; our format choice should be driven by our purposes. For example, if many students are struggling with a particular skill or practice, you might choose to conduct a full-class workshop of only two drafts. This will enable you to engage all students in conversation about this challenge at the same time, using direct examples from student writing. It will also allow you to model response strategies. On the other hand, if your goal is to help students see the variety of ways they might approach a project, you might use peer response groups of four or five students.

Small Groups

Peer response is challenging work, perhaps especially in small groups. Often, students will need a good deal of time (and patience on your part!) to get over their initial shyness, fear that they will offend, lack of confidence, or lack of a shared language with which to discuss writing. Learning to talk about writing is a process in and of itself; it takes time to develop a lexicon for this work, to identify the components of a text, to cultivate the ability to connect impressions to specific moments in the text. We have found it helpful to provide some guidance for students as they begin this work (see Activity 10-1).

In the writer's process toolbox, we offer a general template for setting up peer-response groups. That template does not ask students to use a form or provide them with specific questions. However, at times, it is useful to do so. Activities 10-2 and 10-3 offer some helpful guidelines.

Activity 10-1

Guidelines for Effective Response

- Respond directly to the writer's note; be the kind of reader the writer needs.
- Offer honest feedback that is true to your experience of the text, but which respects the writer's control of the project. Don't be afraid to say what you really think, but always frame your response in respectful ways. There is a big difference between respectfully aggressive readings and disrespectfully mean-spirited readings.
- Be mindful of where the piece is in its development. For instance, don't closely edit a piece that's early in the drafting process.
- Give the writer a sense of what you think the piece says.
- Give the writer a sense of how you experience the piece.
- Ask the writer probing but supportive questions about the text and its subject; aim to keep the writer thinking hard about the nature of his or her task.
- Help the writer imagine potential audiences/purposes for the piece. If the writer knows the audience and purpose for the piece, try to read it with those in mind.
- Aim for both "global" responses that speak to the whole piece and more "local" responses that point to specific places in the text.
- Help the writer see his or her piece from other perspectives.
- Offer the writer a response he or she can handle; don't overwhelm the writer, but be substantive in your response.
- Offer the writer *concrete* suggestions for revision—send him or her back to specific places in the text to do some work.
- Above all, aim to send the writer away from the response session excited about the project and confident that he or she knows where to take it next.

Teaching Writing That Matters © 2008 by Chris W. Gallagher and Amy Lee, Scholastic Professional.

Teaching Writing That Matters

Activity 10-2
Questions for Early Drafts

1. What is the controlling idea of the piece? What makes you think this is the most important idea? How does the writer highlight this idea and build around it?

2. Is this idea worth putting "out there"? Why? What might it add to the discussion of this subject? What could be the effects of sharing this idea with readers?

3. Whom does the piece address? Is this the right readership for this piece? Are these readers best able to address or think about the issues raised? Will they be interested in the piece? Why or why not?

4. What other ways are there of thinking about this subject? What has the writer not considered? How can the writer show that the position in this piece is more appropriate or useful or just plain right than others?

5. Does the form seem appropriate for the intended readers and for this idea/purpose? Why or why not? Comment on the expectations readers are likely to bring to this piece because of its form. (Example: Readers of pamphlets will expect a readable design and quick, concise chunks of information.)

6. How do the different parts of the piece affect you, especially as you imagine yourself as one of the intended readers for the piece? ("As I read the third paragraph, I am frustrated/relieved/interested/confused . . .")

7. What would you (again, imagining yourself as an intended reader) like to hear more about? What could you stand hearing less about? Why? Which ideas could be extended or recast? How?

8. What assumptions does the text make? Are they fair? Accurate? Do they need to be supported? If so, how? If not, what makes you think that readers will be inclined to accept them?

9. Are all of the ideas relevant to one another and to the controlling idea? Is it clear that all of the ideas belong in the same piece? Give an example of how two ideas are either connected or disconnected in the piece. ➜

10. Are the sources well chosen for this readership/purpose/message? Are they authoritative but accessible? Does the writer's use of sources suggest that he or she is knowledgeable about the subject and has something important to add to the discussion? Have you read or heard anything that you think the writer might want to consider?

Teaching Writing That Matters © 2008 by Chris W. Gallagher and Amy Lee, Scholastic Professional.

Activity 10-3
Questions for Later Drafts

1. Is the audience clearly indicated in the piece? How? How are readers drawn in and kept reading? Is the form right for these readers? Why or why not?

2. Are the purpose and the message (controlling idea) clear in the piece? Do they speak to that audience? Is it clear what the writer wants the audience to do/think/believe after reading this piece?

3. What is distinctive about this piece? Does it show creativity? Does it add to the existing conversation about this topic? Explain or give an example.

4. Are the "moves" and appeals made in the text appropriate to the audience? If so, how? If not, why not? Are the intended readers likely to find the idea/argument/story compelling and/or persuasive? Why or why not?

5. Is the piece focused? Are there places where the cohesiveness of the piece breaks down, where the focus is lost? Give examples of where ideas are connected or disconnected in the piece.

6. Is the piece well organized? If so, show how. If not, explain why. Point to specific parts of the text where, for example, the order of paragraphs works well or doesn't—or where sentences build nicely on each other or don't.

7. Is the language appropriate to the audience? Give two examples, either way. ➡

Teaching Writing That Matters

8. Are there grammatical/mechanical problems that need to be addressed? Do you know how to fix them? If not, can you at least point them out? Has the piece been well proofread? Are there obvious spelling or typing errors?

Teaching Writing That Matters © 2008 by Chris W. Gallagher and Amy Lee, Scholastic Professional.

These questions may of course be tailored or simplified. For some peer response groups, we simply ask students to identify two things they like about their peers' drafts and one thing they would change. But whether we provide students with specific questions or not, it is important to discuss with them that drafts at different stages will require different reading and responding practices.

A final note about small-group peer response: some teachers prefer to mix up response groups each time students respond to each other's writing, and other teachers prefer to form permanent groups. Each method has its advantages and disadvantages. Mixing up the groups allows students to work with many of their peers, for example, but it can be a fractured, inefficient experience, as each new group will need time to learn how to work together. On the other hand, permanent groups allow students to build trust and to learn how to support each other, but they can also get stale. As always, the choice depends on your particular students and their specific needs. We do advise asking students to self-monitor their group's functioning, perhaps by asking them for anonymous evaluations of the group every few weeks. Whole-class conversations about what is going well and not so well in groups can also be very helpful.

Resources on Peer Response Groups

Anson, C. (Ed.). (1989). *Writing and response: Theory, practice, research.* Urbana, IL: National Council of Teachers of English.

Brooke, R., Mirtz, R., & Evans, R. (1994). *Small groups in writing workshops.* Urbana, IL: National Council of Teachers of English.

Elbow, P. (1973). *Writing without teachers*. New York: Oxford University Press.

Spear, K. (1988). *Sharing writing: Peer response groups in English classes*. Portsmouth, NH: Heinemann/Boynton/Cook.

Spigelman, C. (2000). *Across property lines: Textual ownership in writing groups*. Carbondale: Southern Illinois University Press.

Whole-Class Workshopping

"Workshop" is a common metaphor to describe the way in which many teachers set up their writing classrooms. The metaphor resonates with teachers because it emphasizes writing as a *craft*—as a process of careful, artful construction—and because it imagines the classroom as a place where craftspeople work together.

So you will hear teachers refer to "a workshop classroom" or "workshop pedagogy" to describe the general approach of a course. Certainly, this book could be used to support "a workshop classroom." In this section, though, we have a different usage of the term *workshop* in mind: the specific classroom practice we call whole-class workshopping.

What It Is

A workshop involves sustained, collective review and response to a single text. You might think of it as a full-class response group. Typically, the text under review was written by a member of the class; however, published texts may also be workshopped.

Why

Workshops generate multiple perspectives on and responses to a text. Workshops nicely supplement peer response groups, providing writers with a broader range of responses. They are a great way to develop a shared vocabulary for talking about writing. They also allow us to "freeze" moments in a text in order to look at them together and learn from them. Workshops are about slowing down writing, paying close attention to what texts say and how they work.

While an individual text is the focus of attention at any given time, workshops are not about "fixing" that text or only providing the writer with feedback. Workshops can benefit all participants because they give everyone a chance to inquire into and talk about writing in process. Ideally, all workshop participants will extract ideas from the workshop and take those back to their own pieces.

Finally, workshops help develop a greater sense of collaboration and community in a class because they depend on the efforts of everyone and because they honor the serious work of writing. Workshops are one of the most effective ways to demonstrate that students' writing is indeed legitimate and meaningful.

How

While all workshops revolve around discussion in response to a text, there are many ways to set up a workshop. Sometimes, readers have had a day or two with the text before the workshop begins; other times, the writer passes out the piece as the workshop commences; still other times, the text is displayed on an overhead or projected on a screen from a computer. Sometimes the writer reads the piece aloud to the group; other times, readers read the text on their own. Sometimes the writer leads discussion with a writer's note; other times the writer only listens. Sometimes an entire class period is given over to a single text; other times, three or four pieces can be handled in that same period of time. Sometimes the teacher (or a student facilitator) will guide discussion, offering specific questions; other times, the discussion develops naturally. Your decisions about how to set up the workshop should be driven by the goals you set for it, as well as contingencies such as the number of students you have, their ability level, the length of projects, the available technologies, and so on.

Tips for Workshopping

- **Explain the purposes of the workshop.** Students are much more likely to work in good faith if they understand *why* they are workshopping. They need the "payoff" for the hard work you're asking them to do. They also learn better (and more) when they clearly understand what it is they're supposed to be learning. A student who thinks workshops are only about giving other people advice, for instance, is likely to miss out on important insights for his or her own writing.

- **Establish a reliable but flexible procedure.** Workshops involve difficult, often touchy work; students appreciate a structure they can rely on, especially as they begin their work together. At the same time, it's important to be open to changes in procedure as the uniqueness of each group becomes apparent.

- **Be patient.** Like writing itself, workshopping is a complex activity. Moreover, students are often hesitant, at first, to give and receive engaged feedback; they need to learn to trust one another (and you). Workshops usually take some time to find their rhythm. Don't be discouraged if conversations don't immediately take off; it might take several workshops before you establish a consistent and effective dynamic. Early on in workshops, you will likely find yourself asking lots of prompting questions: "What is the function of this paragraph about his mother's family?" "Why does she open her essay with a personal memory?" "For whom is this move likely to be effective?" "How will the intended readers likely respond to this example?"

- **Make use of writer's notes.** Writer's notes, remember, are invitations into a piece of writing (see page 128). Often, the best way to get (or keep) students talking about a piece of writing is to point them to the questions the writer has generated about it. This also honors the writer's intentions for and ideas about the text.

- **Try a dry run.** It's helpful to conduct a practice session, perhaps using a piece written by you or by a student you had in a previous class. This allows you to model the kinds of responses you're looking for, while allowing students to become comfortable with the workshop atmosphere and the specific tools you'll ask them to use.

- **Try workshopping a published piece.** Students are often comforted by the knowledge that even published pieces of writing can be treated as in-process. This tends to demystify writing, and to help build student confidence in their ability to respond insightfully to texts.

- **Assign a timekeeper.** This might sound like a minor detail, but it is very easy to lose track of time while workshopping. And doing so can have serious consequences, if a student text is given short shrift, or taken off the agenda altogether. Timekeepers might be asked to signal when there are five minutes left for each project, for instance.

Teaching Writing That Matters

- **Monitor how the workshops are working.** Occasionally, it's useful to step back from the workshop in order to assess what's going well and what's not. How are workshops supporting students' learning? How are they interfering with that learning? What is most useful about workshops? Least useful? Students are often keen observers of classroom dynamics and can offer helpful advice about whether or how to alter the workshop format.

Responding to and Assessing Student Writing

This section is aimed at making visible the different modes of, moments for, and pressures on responding to student writing. When we teach writing, we aim to slow down the process so that developing writers can see the variety of options available to them and learn how to make an effective choice given the specific rhetorical context at work. It is similarly useful for us to slow down and reflect upon our process of responding to students' work. So, this section does not aim to provide you with *the* new and improved version of response. Rather, we're hoping to generate a conversation that you can pursue through observing and reflecting on your practices, or that you might engage in with teaching colleagues. This conversation might aim to:

- Help you identify how and why you currently respond to student writing
- Provide you with more options in responding
- Help you make deliberate choices about how and why to respond in a given moment

Purposes of Responding

As teachers, we provide different kinds of response at different moments. But we might also fall into a kind of "default" mode, working to get through the papers without making a conscious choice about how and why we want to respond to a given assignment. So it might be helpful to identify the two major kinds of response we provide:

- *Formative response* aims primarily to help students develop their writing. Might focus on confidence building, engaging the student in a conversation about her ideas or writing choices in order to help her see herself as a successful and promising writer. Might focus on helping student develop a particular writing project, from one draft to next. Or, might suggest to student some general skills she could focus on developing over the course of a semester.
- *Summative response* focuses on evaluation of how well a student has done. Might be related to a grade. Used primarily on a final product or portfolio. Tends to emphasize whether or not a student has met the criteria operative for a specific assignment and to explain that judgment.

Means of Responding

We respond to many kinds of writing and at different stages in the process, from reading responses, to exercises, to generation or brainstorming, to drafts, to source critiques, to final drafts. It is useful to think carefully about when we want to respond formatively and when we want to respond summatively. It is also helpful to think of the various forms that response can take.

- *Conferencing: verbal, interactive response.* This might happen in class or after class. We can ask students questions about their work, modeling a process of reflecting on and revising a piece of writing. Students can also ask us questions and receive immediate feedback. A conference is typically a formative response mechanism, but might also serve usefully to convey a summative response.
- *Written comments*
  1. *Local:* When we focus on "local" moments in a piece of writing, we are calling attention to specifics in the text. We might note certain patterns of grammar or moments where the piece takes a sudden, unexpected turn. We might also use local comments to emphasize a powerful turn of phrase, or a compelling and well-developed moment. Local commenting

tends to happen in the margins, to call attention to specific moments in the piece by highlighting them and explaining their significance. We tend to use local commenting more often on drafts and when doing formative response.

2. *Global:* When we focus more on the overall piece of writing and less on the specific moments in and of themselves. Global comments tend to come at the end of a piece, in narrative-form response. We might use these to step back and tell the writer what we learned overall, or to comment on a piece's general organizational structure or focus. We tend to use these for a summative response.

3. *Rubrics:* Charts or grids on which we identify the central requirements or goals of a specific project. We evaluate whether or not, and how effectively, students met those criteria. As the next section shows, these can be written *with* students as a means of helping them see and articulate the goals of a given project.

Rubrics: Tools for Response and Assessment

Rubrics are a common but controversial assessment tool. As several of the resources in our sidebar explain, rubrics can be dangerously reductive. They can become nothing more than sorting machines that standardize writing and get in the way of richer, more meaningful teacher and reader response. This is of course the opposite of what we want in a Writing Studies classroom, in which our first goal is to send students the message that someone on the other side of the page cares about what they have to say. When rubrics are used only to assign students numbers, they are counterproductive.

But under certain conditions, we believe rubrics can play a role in Writing Studies classrooms. They can help us articulate clear expectations for writers and provide shared language that we and our students can use to deepen and extend our discussions about writing. They may also be used by students to self-assess or to evaluate each other's writing. In short, they can become a community tool for teaching and learning writing.

However, to experience the benefits of rubrics without incurring the serious drawbacks—most seriously, the stifling of student creativity—we offer the following suggestions:

1. Create rubrics *with* students; make sure the rubric reflects the values, goals, and language of this writing community.

2. Generate rubrics only *after* students have drafted. Rubrics should function descriptively, not prescriptively. They can help students see the extent to which they are achieving their own goals—but they should not be slavishly followed.

3. Ask students to use rubrics to assess their own work and that of peers. Use disagreements in evaluations as a prompt for discussion; never sacrifice conversation for reader agreement.

4. Ensure that rubrics are flexible enough to include criteria that individual students might find important to consider even if the group does not. (You might consider having a "wild card" category, for example.)

5. Ensure that rubrics allow for narrative comments, even if it's just in a "notes" column. Again, numbers should not stand in for discursive response; at their best, they can supplement it. (Turley & Gallagher, 2008)

Resources on Rubrics

Broad, B. (2003). *What we really value: Beyond rubrics in teaching and assessing writing.* Logan, UT: Utah State University Press.

Kohn, A. (2006). The trouble with rubrics. *English Journal 95*(4), 12–15.

Spandel, V. (2006). In defense of rubrics. *English Journal 96*(1), 19–22.

Turley, E., & Gallagher, C. (2008). On the uses of rubrics: Framing the great rubric debate. *English Journal 97*(4), 87–92.

Wilson, M. (2006). *Rethinking rubrics in writing assessment.* Portsmouth, NH: Heinemann.

Wilson, M. (2007.) Why I won't be using rubrics to respond to students' writing. *English Journal* 96(4), 62–66.

Rubrics are time-consuming to develop, but the process has many benefits. Most importantly, it helps students connect to the work of the project and approach it reflectively. Here is a template for how you might co-construct rubrics with your students during a writing project:

1. After students have written their first drafts, ask them to generate a list of goals for their projects. You might begin with a writing prompt or with small groups. For example, if students were working on a family/community history project, you might ask, "What does an effective family/community history project include? How will we know you've done a good job?" Consider whether you will include only product descriptors (textual features) or process features (extent of revisions, ability to self-reflect, etc.). Writing Studies classrooms typically include attention to both product and process.

2. Capture the goals on which the group can arrive at consensus; be clear that these goals will become the evaluative criteria for the projects. Sometimes, criteria will need to be reworded or combined. You may have some bottom-line criteria that you believe must make the final cut (including criteria predetermined by district or state requirements); that's fine, as long as students also have a say. In the end, you want to identify between five and seven criteria.

3. On your own, create a set of performance-level descriptors, using whatever classification system makes sense—traditional A–F grades, a numbering system such as 1–4 or 1–6, adjectives such as *poor, fair, good, exceptional*, and so on. (This may be done with students as well, but in our experience, this step is extremely difficult to complete via a "live" consensus process.) For each category, be as clear as you can about how performance at each level would differ from performance at the other levels. How would an "A" project be different from a "B" project? How would a "3" project differ from a "2" project? Some of

these gradations may be precise; for example the number of reading responses students hand in determines their performance level. Other times—probably most times—they will require a value judgment: the determination of the difference between "effective, substantive revisions," for example, and "mechanical, minimal revisions."

4. Bring the draft rubric to class and have students review it and make recommendations on how to improve it. This process of co-constructing rubrics helps students not only to understand the expectations, but also to have some investment in them, as they originate not only from the teacher in seemingly arbitrary fashion but also from the will of the writing community.

5. Ask students to use their rubrics to guide revision. At the completion of the project, you and students may use the rubrics to rate their work either analytically (i.e., by category) or holistically. Importantly, the rubrics should become prompts for discussion between and among you and your students.

Sample Narrative Rubric for Writing With Research Project

An "A" project clearly and compellingly demonstrates how the public event influenced the family. It shows strong audience awareness, engaging readers throughout. The form and structure are appropriate for the purpose(s) and audience(s) of the piece. The final product is virtually error-free. The piece seamlessly weaves in relevant research. Drafts show extensive, effective revision. Writer's notes and final learning letter demonstrate thoughtful reflection and growing awareness of the writer's strengths and challenges.

A "B" project clearly and compellingly demonstrates how the public event influenced the family. It shows strong audience awareness, and usually engages readers. The form and structure are appropriate for the audience(s) and purpose(s) of the piece, though the organization may not be tight in a couple of places. The final product includes a few errors, but these do no interfere with readers' comprehension. The piece effectively, if not always seamlessly, weaves in relevant research. Drafts show extensive, effective revision.

Writer's notes and final learning letter demonstrate thoughtful reflection and growing awareness of the writer's strengths and challenges.

A "C" project demonstrates how the public event influenced the family. It shows audience awareness, sometimes engaging readers. The form and structure are appropriate for the audience(s) and purpose(s), but the organization breaks down at times. The piece includes several obvious errors, which at times compromise the comprehensibility of the piece. The piece incorporates relevant research, but in a generally forced or awkward way. There is unevenness in the quality and appropriateness of the research. Drafts show some evidence of revision. Writer's notes and final learning letter show some reflection and growth in awareness of the writer's strengths and challenges.

A "D" project discusses a public event and a family, but the connections may not be clear. It shows little audience awareness. The form and structure are poorly chosen or poorly executed. The piece includes many errors, which regularly compromise the comprehensibility of the piece. There is an attempt to incorporate research, but this is done awkwardly or is drawn from incomplete or inappropriate research. There is little evidence of revision. Writer's notes and learning letter are missing or show little reflection or growth.

An "F" project is not responsive to the prompt. It shows little or no audience awareness. The audience and purpose are unclear, and the form and structure are poorly chosen and poorly executed. The piece includes many errors, compromising the comprehensibility of the piece throughout. There is little or no evidence of research. There is little or no evidence of revision. Writer's notes and learning letter are missing or show no reflection or growth.

Sample Chart Rubric for Community/Family History Project

	A	B	C	D	F	Wild Card
Ideas	Clearly and compellingly demonstrates influence of event	Clearly and compellingly demonstrates influence of event	Demonstrates influence of event	Discusses event; connections unclear	Not responsive to prompt	
Audience	Strong audience awareness; engages throughout	Strong audience awareness; usually engages	Audience awareness; sometimes engages	Little audience awareness	Little or no audience awareness	
Form/Structure	Appropriate for audience(s), purpose(s)	Appropriate for audience(s), purpose(s); organization occasionally not tight	Appropriate for audience(s), purpose(s); organization breaks down at times	Poorly chosen or poorly executed	Poorly chosen and executed	
Conventions	Virtually error-free	Few, unobtrusive errors	Several obvious, sometimes obtrusive errors	Many obtrusive errors	Many obtrusive errors	

	A	**B**	**C**	**D**	**F**	**Wild Card**
Research	Seamlessly weaves in research; uses relevant and effective sources	Effectively weaves in research; one source may not be as relevant or effective	Incorporates research, but awkwardly; has too few sources or sources that aren't relevant	Attempts to incorporate research, but awkwardly; poor research	Little or no evidence of research	
Revision	Extensive, effective	Extensive, effective	Some evidence of revision	Little evidence of revision	No evidence of revision	
Reflection	Thoughtful reflection; growing self-awareness	Thoughtful reflection; growing self-awareness	Some evidence of reflection, growth	Little evidence of reflection	Little or no evidence of reflection	

Using Readings to Teach Writing

The question of readings—why we include them, what to do with them, how to choose them—is an ongoing negotiation for many of us in our writing classes. Indeed, we find this question visited and revisited in Writing Studies scholarship. For us, the main question is how to help students read in ways that stimulate, support, and inspire their own writing.

Reading Rhetorically, or Reading as a Writer

Typically, the content model dominates our English classes. In this familiar model, texts are chosen primarily for the ideas, information, or images they deliver with little attention to *how* they do so. The content model, to our thinking, introduces an unproductive contradiction: students are asked to read "professional" writing for *what* it says, while ignoring *how* and *why* it was composed; such attention to the act and process of writing is reserved for their own work. We worry that this model further reinforces the false distinctions between "student" writers (who must work at writing) and "real" writers (who already know how to write) by treating professional texts as artifacts that were not purposefully and intentionally composed, or as texts that are not affected by the rhetorical context in which they are read.

The alternative model that informs this book is what we call reading as a writer, or rhetorical reading. In this model, we engage readings with attention not only to what a text is saying but to how it is composed (the choices a writer makes); in other words, we emphasize the need to study both the way the text works and the work the text does in the world. In a sense, reading rhetorically means reading *behind* the words on the page, looking both at the micro-workings of the language and the macro-workings of the contexts in which the language circulates. Reading rhetorically does not necessitate that we ignore the content of the text; it is not a matter of trading content for composition, but rather of multiple emphases and increased potential benefits. In our experience, as students learn to read texts with an eye to understanding the relationship between how they are composed, the operative rhetorical context, and what makes them effective or not, they gain knowledge about written communication that they can use in their own writing. They also deepen their practice of critical, active reading.

Invitations Into Reading

If we want students to read as writers, we will need to help them learn how to do this work. Vague or general assignments ("Turn in a $1\frac{1}{2}$-page response to the text") tend to invite vague and general responses ("I liked it"; "It was boring"). At the same time, if we create response assignments that are too prescriptive or directive, we risk foreclosing the possibility for students to actively engage the text by questioning, discovering, analyzing, and connecting its key components. When we are creating reading work for our students, whether choosing texts or writing assignments, we find it helps to ask ourselves: "What kind of work do I want students to do and how will this text allow for that? What are my purposes for them (as readers? as writers?) in asking them to work with this text? How can they engage in conversation with the text, as both readers and writers?"

Obviously, these are different kinds of questions from those that inform a more content-based use of texts. In a content model, you might choose texts according to ideas you want to expose students to, or according to a theme you want to build through the semester, or in order to include a range of voices and perspectives. You might still consider these factors in a rhetorical reading-oriented class. Again, this is not a matter of trading or choosing between, but of synthesizing. So, for instance, you might choose to use three texts that take up the same topic in different rhetorical contexts, speaking to distinct audiences, in a range of forms, using various strategies.

We certainly don't mean to suggest this is easy work for teachers. Often, we need to experiment with a given assignment: test it out, reflect on its value and success, refine and revise it the next time around. As we discussed at the beginning of this toolbox, reflective practice is about ongoing reflection and revision—having a rationale or purpose that guides our choices, being attuned to what happens in practice, and being willing to revise. In this way, as we've suggested before, teaching is a process akin to the writing process in which we hope to engage our students.

To help illustrate how to encourage students to do rhetorical reading, or to read as writers, we have included some sample assignments (Activities 10-4 through 10-6), along with references to specific texts. Please note, however, that we have chosen these particular texts for illustrative purposes only; these reading activities can be used with a wide range of texts—including students' own writing. In any case, these activities demonstrate a range of options—from those that focus close scrutiny on a particular component of the text to those that step back to reflect on a text's overall workings.

Activity 10-4
Structuring Meaning

(Based on an excerpt from Talking to High Monks in the Snow *by Lydia Yuri Minatoya)*

1. **Glossing:** As you look at the physical layout of Minatoya's text, you'll notice that it is divided into sections through the use of larger amounts of white space between certain paragraphs. Minatoya's memoir seems to offer visual clues—via the arrangement of the text on the page—to guide us through the narrative. Using these divisions, look at each section and make a note about what you think that section of the text is doing, what its main idea is, what it is suggesting. Pause after each section, look at any marginal notes you made while reading, and ask whichever of these questions make the most sense to you: What is the message in this section? What is the mood? What purpose does this section serve? What truth is suggested by this section?

2. Now that you have looked closely at each section, including the final scene, think about how the sections relate to each other. What connections can you make between the sections? Are there gaps or jumps? If so, what purpose do they serve? Are ideas repeated or echoed in different sections? Be specific with examples as you answer these questions.

3. Finally, think again about what themes have been built up and developed throughout the piece. How does your examination of each section help you gain a deeper understanding of the complete text?

Teaching Writing That Matters © 2008 by Chris W. Gallagher and Amy Lee, Scholastic Professional.

Getting the Message

(Based on Mark Twain's "Reading the River" and Jamaica Kincaid's A Small Place)

The *what* of these pieces (the message or significance communicated) is intricately related to the *how* of these essays (the techniques the writer uses, the language, voice, flow, and so on). In this activity, we are going to look at both what these writers are trying to tell us as well as how they go about doing it.

1. Before we look at how these pieces work, let's spend some time thinking about what they are trying to do. For each essay, Kincaid's and Twain's, write a paragraph explaining what deeper significance the writer is trying to communicate. So Twain is writing about a river, but what is his underlying message? Kincaid is describing Antigua, but what ideas is she communicating beyond aspects of the place?

2. One of the central techniques used throughout Twain's essay is an extended metaphor: the river is a book that one learns to read and, later, to reread. That is, like a book read repeatedly, the river takes on new meaning according to the reader's situation or perspective. To make an extended metaphor work in a piece, the writer must weave it in throughout the text. So, find at least three places where Twain is working this metaphor. Write down these three passages and explain how they help develop his message—how do these moments of metaphor help us understand his point?

3. Kincaid uses several rhetorical techniques in her essay. Identify one of these techniques (for example, showing rather than telling, repetition, irony) and cite a couple of passages where you see it being used. Then explain what effect you think this technique has on the text—how does it impact her essay? How does it help her to better communicate her point?

Attending to Openings

(Based on Amy Tan's "Mother Tongue")

Openings are important elements in any form of writing. How a piece begins influences the reader's first impression of the narrator or speaker, of what is to come in the piece, and even whether or not to keep reading. In the conventions of academic writing, we do not often think of beginning by refuting our authority. Nonetheless, Amy Tan begins "Mother Tongue" by claiming she is not a scholar and can offer you no more than "personal opinions." But notice the second line ("I am a writer") and how it serves as a declarative statement that gives her authority, of a different sort than "scholarly," in relation to her topic.

So, why does Tan begin this way? In other words, what is the intended effect of this rhetorical strategy? Think about how this opening influences your first impression of the piece—what does it lead you to expect from the essay, of the narrator? Finally, is this impression effective in setting up the rest of the piece? Does it work in relation to her purpose and message?

Teaching Writing That Matters © 2008 by Chris W. Gallagher and Amy Lee, Scholastic Professional.

References

Allison, D. (1996). *Two or three things I know for sure*. New York: Penguin.

Berthoff, A. E. (1981). *The making of meaning*. Montclair, NJ: Boynton/Cook.

Bishop, W., & Strickland, J. (Eds.). (2006). *The subject is writing* (4th ed.). Portsmouth, NH: Boynton/Cook.

Brandt, D. (1990). *Literacy as involvement: The acts of writers, readers, and texts*. Carbondale: Southern Illinois University Press.

Brodkey, L. (1996). *Writing permitted in designated areas only*. Minneapolis, MN: University of Minnesota Press.

Brooke, R., & McIntosh, J. (2007). Deep maps: Teaching rhetorical engagement through place-conscious education. In C. Keller & C. Weisser (Eds.). *The locations of composition* (pp. 131–149). Albany: SUNY Press.

Bruffee, K. A. (1993). *A short course in writing: Composition, collaborative learning, and constructive reading* (4th ed.). New York: HarperCollins.

Dewey, J. (1933). *How we think*. Boston: Heath.

———. (1899/1956). *The school and society*. Chicago: University of Chicago Press.

———. (1916/1966). *Democracy and education*. New York: Free Press.

Dillard, A. (1989). *The writing life*. New York: Harper & Row.

Downs, D., & Wardle, E. (2007). Teaching about writing, righting misconceptions: (Re)envisioning "first-year composition" as "introduction to writing studies." *College Composition and Communication, 58* (4), 552–584.

Elbow, P. (1973). *Writing without teachers*. New York: Oxford University Press.

———. (1998). *Writing with power*. (2nd ed.). New York: Oxford University Press.

Epstein, J. (1995). *With my trousers rolled: Familiar essays*. New York: Norton.

Fadiman, A. (2007). *At large and at small: Familiar essays*. New York: Farrar, Straus and Giroux.

Faulkner, W. (1973). The bear. In *Go down, Moses* (pp. 191–334). New York: Vintage.

Fink, L. D. (2003). *Creating significant learning experiences*. San Francisco: Jossey-Bass.

Freire, P. (2000). *Pedagogy of the oppressed*. New York: Continuum International Publishing.

Gallagher, C. W. (2007). *Reclaiming assessment: A better alternative to the accountability agenda*. Portsmouth, NH: Heinemann.

Goodburn, A. (2001). Writing the public sphere through family/community history. *Readerly/Writerly Texts*, 9.1 and 9.2 (Spring/Summer 2001 and Fall/Winter 2001): 9–24.

Goodlad, J. (1984). *A place called school: Prospects for the future*. New York: McGraw-Hill.

Graff, G. (2003). *Clueless in academe*. New Haven, CT: Yale University Press.

Graham, S., & Perin, D. (2006). *Writing next*. New York: Carnegie Foundation Alliance for Excellent Education.

Hargreaves, A. (1995). *Changing teachers, changing times*. Ontario: Ontario Institute for Studies in Education.

Hillocks, G., Jr. (2002). *The testing trap*. New York: Teachers College Press.

hooks, b. (1994). *Teaching to transgress*. New York: Routledge.

Kincaid, J. (2000). *A small place*. New York: Farrar, Straus and Giroux.

Lamott, A. (1994). *Bird by bird: Some instructions on writing and life*. New York: Anchor.

Lecourt, D., and the UMass Writing Collective. (2005). *The text-wrestling book*. Dubuque, IA: Kendall-Hunt.

McNeil, L. (2000). *Contradictions of reform: The educational costs of standardized testing*. New York: Routledge.

Meier, D. (2002). *In schools we trust*. Boston: Beacon Press.

Minatoya, L. Y. (1992). *Talking to high monks in the snow: An Asian American odyssey*. New York: HarperCollins.

Murray, D. M. (1972). Teach writing as process not product. *The Leaflet, 71* (3), 11–14.

Nagin, C., & The National Writing Project. (2003). *Because writing matters*. San Francisco: Jossey-Bass.

National Commission on Writing. (2003). *The neglected "R": The need for a writing revolution*. Retrieved January 9, 2008, from http://www.writingcommission.org.

———. (2004). *Writing: A ticket to work or a ticket out*. Retrieved January 9, 2008, from http://www.writingcommission.org.

———. (2005). *Writing: A powerful message from state government*. Retrieved January 9, 2008, from http://www.writingcommission.org.

———. (2006). *Writing and school reform*. Retrieved January 9, 2008, from http://www.writingcommission.org.

Nebraska Department of Education. (2001). *Statewide writing assessment scoring guide*. Lincoln, NE: Author.

Nystrand, M. (1997). *Opening dialogue: Understanding the dynamics of language and learning in the English classroom*. New York: Teachers College Press.

O'Neill, P., Crow, A., & Burton, L. W. (2002). *A field of dreams: Independent writing programs and the future of composition*. Logan, UT: Utah State University Press.

Rich, A. (2001a). The arts of the possible. In *Arts of the possible: Essays and conversation* (pp. 146–167). New York: Norton.

———. (2001b). When we dead awaken. In *Arts of the possible: Essays and conversation* (pp. 10–29). New York: Norton.

Ritchie, J. S., & Wilson, D. E. (2000). *Teacher narrative as critical inquiry: rewriting the script.* New York: Teachers College Press.

Salvatori, M., & Donahue, P. A. (2005). *The elements (and pleasures) of difficulty.* New York: Longman.

Schön, D. A. (1987). *Educating the reflective practitioner: Toward a new design for teaching and learning in the professions.* San Francisco: Jossey-Bass.

Shamoon, L. K., Howard, R. M., Jamieson, S., & Schwegler, R. A. (Eds.). (2000). *Coming of age: The advanced writing curriculum.* Portsmouth, NH: Boynton/Cook.

Sizer, T. (1984). *Horace's compromise: The dilemma of the American high school.* Boston: Houghton Mifflin.

Tan, A. (2006). Mother tongue. In D. McQuade & R. Atwan (Eds.). *The writer's presence: A pool of readings* (pp. 290–295). New York: Bedford St. Martin's.

Twain, M. (1911/1950). *Life on the Mississippi.* New York: Harper and Brothers.

Welch, N. (1997). *Getting restless: Rethinking revision in writing instruction.* Portsmouth, NH: Boynton/Cook.

Welch, N. (2005). Living room: Teaching public writing in a post-publicity era. *College composition and communication, 56* (3), 470–492.

Wiggins, G. P., & McTighe, J. (2005). *Understanding by design* (2nd ed.). Upper Saddle River, NJ: Prentice-Hall.

Williams, J. M. (1981). The phenomenology of error. *College Composition and Communication, 32* (2), 152–168.

Wilson, D. E. (1994). *Attempting change: Teachers moving from writing project to classroom practice.* Portsmouth, NH: Boynton/Cook.

Index